St. John Paul II Edition—Updated, Revised, and Expanded

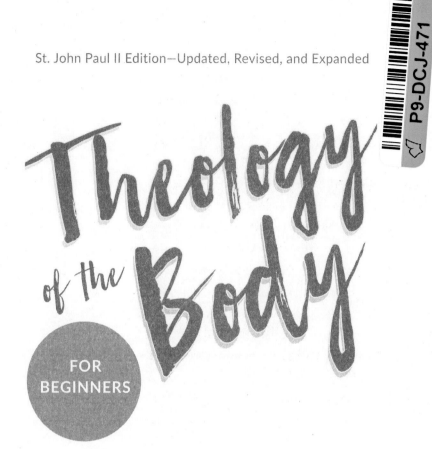

Theology of the Body

of the

FOR BEGINNERS

Rediscovering the Meaning of
Life, Love, Sex, and Gender

CHRISTOPHER WEST

WELLSPRING
North Palm Beach, Florida

Published by Wellspring
All rights reserved.

Design: Ashley Wirfel

ISBN 978-1-63582-007-2 (softcover)
ISBN 978-1-929266-45-6 (e-book)

Library of Congress Cataloging-in-Publication Data
Names: West, Christopher, 1969- author.
Title: Theology of the body for beginners : rediscovering the meaning of life, love, sex, and gender / Christopher West.
Description: St. John Paul II Edition. |
North Palm Beach, Florida : Beacon Publishing, 2018.
Identifiers: LCCN 2017054247 | ISBN 9781635820072 (softcover) |
ISBN 9781929266456 (e-book)
Subjects: LCSH: John Paul II, Pope, 1920-2005. Theology of the body. |
Human body—Religious aspects—Catholic Church. | Theological anthropology—Catholic Church.
Classification: LCC BX1795.B63 J6638 2018 | DDC
233/.5—dc23

Dynamic Catholic® and Be Bold. Be Catholic.®
and The Best Version of Yourself® are registered trademarks of The Dynamic Catholic Institute.

For more information on this title or other books and CDs available through the Dynamic Catholic Book Program, please visit www.DynamicCatholic.com.

The Dynamic Catholic Institute
5081 Olympic Blvd • Erlanger • Kentucky • 41018
Phone: 1–859–980–7900
Email: info@DynamicCatholic.com

10   9   8   7   6

Printed in Italy

Other Books by
CHRISTOPHER WEST

Good News about Sex & Marriage:
Answers to Your Honest Questions about Catholic Teaching

Theology of the Body Explained:
A Commentary on John Paul II's Man and Woman He Created Them

The Love That Satisfies:
Reflections on Eros and Agape

Heaven's Song:
Sexual Love as It Was Meant to Be

At the Heart of the Gospel:
Reclaiming the Body for the New Evangelization

Fill These Hearts:
God, Sex, and the Universal Longing

Pope Francis to Go:
Bite-Sized Morsels from The Joy of the Gospel

Love is Patient, but I'm Not:
Confessions of a Recovering Perfectionist

Theology of the Body at the Movies

Table of Contents

INTRODUCTION

*[Christ wants us to] experience that fullness of "eros," which implies
the upward impulse of the human spirit toward what is true, good, and
beautiful, so that what is "erotic" also becomes true, good, and beautiful.*
—St. John Paul II

Sex—that exhilaratingly beautiful, heart-waking and heart-breaking conundrum of human existence! Without a doubt, it's the force that has compelled me on my search for real meaning in life and, to my great surprise, after several years away, led me back into the heart of the Catholic Church. Let me explain.

Desire—eros, or erotic desire, to be more specific—kicked in pretty early in my life. I was often overwhelmed by a gnawing hunger and thirst I didn't know how to handle. God bless my parents, pastors, and Catholic schoolteachers—they all tried their best—but people can't give what they don't have. No one had formed them in the true beauty and splendor of God's plan for erotic desire, so they couldn't form me. I was given the Catholic "rules" about sex, and my teachers did their best to instill a fear in me of breaking them, but I was never given the "why" behind the "what" of the Church's teaching.

Okay, you've given me the rules, but what the heck am I supposed to do with all this desire inside me? The basic message in the air was that my desires were "bad" and needed to be repressed or otherwise squelched. If this was authentic Catholicism, it seemed that the only thing the Church had to offer me in my hunger was a starvation diet. Eventually the hunger became so intense that it trumped all fear of breaking the rules. As I wrote in my book *Fill These Hearts: God, Sex, and the Universal Longing*:

> A person can starve himself for only so long before the choice becomes clear: either I find something to eat, or . . . I'm gonna die. . . . This is why the culture's "fast-food gospel"—the promise of immediate gratification through indulgence of desire—inevitably wins large numbers of converts from the "starvation diet gospel."[1]

Of course, it's equally true that a person can eat "fast food" for only so long before all the grease and sodium take their toll. Once the initial pleasure of filling your belly wears off, bad food, I came to learn, is no less destructive than malnutrition.

Were these the only two options for my hunger: death by starvation or death by food poisoning? Was there any good food to be had, food that could actually bring life to my aching soul? I wanted answers. I *needed* answers! If God were real, I figured he must have some kind of plan for making us this way. So in a college dorm in 1988, I let loose a rather desperate cry of my heart, a ragged prayer that went something like this:

> God in heaven, if you exist, you better show me! And you better show me what this whole sex thing is all about and why you gave me all

these desires, because they're getting me and everybody I know into a hell of a lot of trouble. What is your plan? Do you have a plan? Show me! Please! Show me!

The answer to my prayer came as an interior call that I couldn't ignore: "Seek and you will find . . ." So I turned to the Bible. I figured if this were really God's Word, it had to have something to say about why he made us sexual beings. Over a period of about three years of intense searching and study, I came to see that the Bible takes us on a journey from a wedding in the temporal paradise of Eden to a wedding in the eternal paradise of heaven. I discovered that the prophets used some bold sexual imagery in describing divine love (i.e., Ezekiel 16:7–8), the erotic love poetry of the Song of Songs was a window into the things of heaven, and the one-flesh union of spouses was a "great mystery" that revealed Christ's love for the Church (see Ephesians 5:31–32).

The spousal imagery of the Scriptures was bringing to life the dry doctrine I had learned growing up and was shedding a bright light on the entire Christian mystery. Yes, yes—as I was beginning to discover, there *was* more than the "starvation diet" and "fast food"! This maddening ache I felt inside was a yearning for the infinite, and God put it there to lead me to him! My impression growing up was wrong: Christ doesn't want us to *repress* our desires, he wants to *redeem* our desires—to heal them, to redirect them toward an infinite banquet of love and ecstatic bliss called "the marriage feast of the Lamb" (Revelation 19:9). Discovering this set me on fire!

Expecting an enthusiastic response from other Catholics I knew, I was surprised to be met with blank stares or worse when

I tried to explain how the union of man and woman was like a key that unlocked the mysteries of our faith. Then, in September 1993, a fateful meeting with my sister's high school theology teacher literally changed the course of my life. Testing some of my "spousal" reading of the Bible on her, she responded with, "You must have read John Paul II's Theology of the Body."

"What's that?" I probed.

"Gosh, I thought you'd already read it. What you're saying sounds just like the pope."

I could hardly believe my ears.

Turns out, John Paul II had spent the first major teaching project of his pontificate unfolding an in-depth examination of the very same Scripture passages I had been studying. Reading his Theology of the Body for the first time, I found confirmation that I wasn't crazy, and his insights, not surprisingly, took me to an entirely new level. I sensed I was holding the answer to the crisis of modern times in my hands, and I knew then that I would spend the rest of my life studying his teaching and sharing it with others. Hence began my life's work as a "theologian of the body."

The Masterwork of a Great Saint

I was presenting the final talk of a seminar on John Paul II's Theology of the Body on April 2, 2005, when a participant, reading a message on his cell phone, interrupted me. "The pope just died," he whispered. I shared the news with my audience. We all paused and prayed, and then I somberly concluded the seminar.

Afterward, amid various condolences, someone wondered aloud, "Gee, whatta ya gonna do now?"—as if my life's work had just died along with the pope.

"This isn't the end," I responded without hesitation. "This is just the beginning!" As with the teaching of all the great saint-theologians of history, I knew the Church would be spending centuries unpacking John Paul II's teaching.

At the time of his death, his Theology of the Body (henceforth, TOB) was already creating a buzz in the Church. Today, there are multiple conferences, seminars, study groups, courses, books, and educational resources on the subject available from a great many teachers and authors. Various ministries have arisen to spread the TOB, and interest has extended beyond Catholic borders. Christians of various denominations are discovering in John Paul II's teaching a much-needed biblical response to the sexual revolution and are spreading its message of healing and redemption in their own faith communities. Even so, for the vast majority of Christians, the content of the TOB remains an untapped treasure. The Church's recognition of John Paul II as a saint will certainly help to change that.

The St. John Paul II Edition of This Work

The canonization of John Paul II on April 27, 2014, was more than the Church's official recognition of his heroic virtue. It also cast his teaching, for all of history, in a more radiant and compelling light. His TOB—which, in the words of Professor Michael Waldstein, stands out as "Mount Everest among the hills" in all that John Paul II gave us—is not only the teaching of a wise and learned pope (thus falling under the mantle of "papal authority"). The TOB can now also be understood, received, and embraced as the masterwork of perhaps the greatest saint of modern times.

On the feast day of St. John Paul II (October 22), the Church prays in her liturgy:

> O God, who are rich in mercy
> and who willed that Saint John Paul the Second
> should preside as pope over your universal Church,
> grant, we pray, that instructed by his teaching,
> we may open our hearts to the saving grace of Christ . . .

That is the sole goal of this book: that, instructed by St. John Paul II's teaching, we may open our hearts to the saving grace of Christ.

John Paul II's canonization is reason enough for a fresh look at the TOB. Still, there are other reasons for a new and expanded edition of this work. Since *Theology of the Body for Beginners* was first published in 2004, ongoing study, teaching, writing, and life experience—especially struggles with my own weaknesses as a husband and father striving to live the TOB—have given me a more refined vantage point from which to present the material. Furthermore, cultural attitudes have shifted dramatically since the first edition of this work and need to be addressed with clarity and compassion. In a world of government-enforced gender confusion, John Paul II's insights into the essential meaning and nature of the sexual difference are as timely as they are urgent. Finally, since the pontificates of Pope Benedict XVI and Pope Francis have both contributed to our understanding of John Paul II's teaching, you will see their wisdom integrated throughout this new edition.

After laying an important foundation in chapter one, I introduce the main ideas of John Paul II's teaching according to the structure of his original manuscript. The resource section following the conclusion offers suggestions for continuing your exploration of the "great mystery" into which the TOB plunges us.

I pray that this book helps open a new world for you. Indeed, if we take this great saint's theological vision of our bodies to heart, we will never see ourselves, others, the world around us, the Church, indeed, the whole universe the same way again.

St. John Paul II, pray for us!

ONE

What Is the Theology of the Body?

God impressed his own form on the flesh . . . in such a way that
even what was visible might bear the divine form.
—*St. Irenaeus*

It was a gorgeous, starlit night. A young couple, madly in love, drove off into the country to find a secluded place where they could express their amorous desires. Spotting a grassy knoll, they parked on the side of the road, grabbed a blanket and headed for the far side of the hill.

Little did they know they were on the property of a country parish. An elderly monsignor, hearing some commotion, looked out his rectory window, gathered what was happening, and decided he would go for a little "prayer walk." The young lovers, engrossed as they were in one another, had no idea someone had approached and was now standing at the edge of their blanket. Jolted out of their passion by a startling but nonetheless polite "Excuse me," they were all the more startled by the sight of his Roman collar. Expecting he would scold them roundly, instead, the mysterious man in black looked toward the heavens and probed inquisitively, "Tell me, what does what you're doing *here* have to do with . . . *the stars?*" After a pregnant pause, he walked back to his rectory leaving the dumbfounded lovers to ponder his question.[2]

St. John Paul II, in his own way, invites us to ponder the same question in his extended reflections on the "great mystery" of our creation as male and female and the call of the two to become "one flesh."

The Wednesday Talks

When Karol Wojtyla, the cardinal archbishop of Krakow, came to Rome in August 1978 to help elect a new pope, he brought along the lengthy handwritten manuscript of a book that he had been prayerfully crafting for nearly four years. It was almost complete, and he wished to work on it, when he could, during the conclave. Page one bore the unusual title (in Polish): *"teologia ciala"*—"theology of the body." The hundreds of pages that followed held perhaps the most profound and compelling biblical reflection on the meaning of our creation and redemption as male and female ever articulated—in-depth mystical insights of a modern saint that had the power to change the world . . . *if* those insights had an opportunity to reach the world, that is.

After the election of Pope John Paul I, Wojtyla returned to Krakow and completed his manuscript. Soon after that, to the astonishment of the whole world, he emerged from the second conclave of 1978 as Pope John Paul II. And his "theology of the body"—delivered as a series of 129[3] Wednesday talks between September 1979 and November 1984 rather than being published as a book—became the first major teaching project of his pontificate, establishing the core of John Paul II's great vision of what it means to be human.

Still, it took some time for people to grasp the significance of what John Paul II had given us. It wasn't until 1999, for example, that papal biographer George Weigel described the TOB to a wide readership as "one of the boldest reconfigurations of Catholic theology in centuries" and "a kind of *theological time bomb* set to go off, with dramatic consequences, . . . perhaps in the twenty-first century." While the pope's vision of the body and of sexual love had "barely begun to shape the Church's theology, preaching, and religious education," Weigel predicted that when it did it would "compel a dramatic development of thinking about virtually every major theme in the Creed."[4]

God, Sex, and the Meaning of Life

What might the human body have to do with the tenets of the Christian Creed? To ask questions about the meaning of the body starts us on an exhilarating journey that, if we stay the course, leads us from the body to the mystery of sexual difference; from sexual difference to the mystery of communion in "one flesh"; from the communion in "one flesh" to the mystery of Christ's communion with the Church; and from the communion of Christ and the Church to the greatest mystery of all: the eternal communion found in God among Father, Son, and Holy Spirit. This is what the tenets of the Creed are all about.

The body is not only *bio*logical. The body, as John Paul II unfolds in great detail, is also *theo*logical. It tells an astounding divine story. And it does so precisely through the mystery of sexual difference and the call of the two to become "one flesh." This means that sex is not just about sex. The way we understand and express our sexuality points to our deepest-held convictions about who we are, who God is, the meaning of love, the ordering of society, and, ultimately, the mystery of the universe. Hence, John Paul II's TOB is much more than a reflection on sex and married love. Through that, it leads us to "the rediscovery of the meaning of the whole of existence . . . the meaning of life" (TOB 46:6).

Christ teaches that the meaning of life is found by loving as he loves (see John 15:12). One of John Paul II's main insights is that God inscribed this vocation to love as he loves right *in our bodies* by creating us male and female and calling us to become "one flesh" (see Genesis 2:24). Far from being a footnote in the Christian life, the way we understand the body and the sexual relationship "concerns the whole Bible" (TOB 69:8). It plunges us into "the perspective of the whole gospel, of the whole teaching, even more, of the whole mission of Christ" (TOB 49:3).

Christ's mission is to restore the order of love in a world seriously distorted by sin. And the union of the sexes, as always, lies at the basis of the human "order of love." Therefore, what we learn in John Paul II's TOB is obviously "important with regard to marriage." However it "is equally essential and *valid for the [understanding] of man* in general: for the fundamental problem of understanding him and for the self-understanding of his being in the world" (TOB, 102:5).

Are you looking for the meaning of life? Are you looking to understand the fundamental questions of existence? Our bodies tell the story. But we must learn how to "read" that story properly, and this is not easy. A great many obstacles, prejudices, and fears can derail us as we seek to enter the "great mystery" of our own embodiment as male and female. For religious people, the most common temptation is to reject the body as "unspiritual."

Christianity Does Not Reject the Body

Religious people are used to an emphasis on "spiritual" things. However, many are unfamiliar, and sometimes very uncomfortable, with an emphasis on the body. But this reveals a very dangerous split or dualism in our thinking. Spirit has a certain priority over matter, since God, in himself, is pure spirit. Yet God is the author of the physical world, and in his wisdom, he did not make us pure spirits. He made us as *incarnate spirits*: a physical and spiritual unity.

Living a "spiritual life" as a Christian *never* means splitting off from the physical world. Jesus "was far removed from philosophies which despised the body, matter, and the things of the world," insists Pope Francis. Yet he also recognizes that such "unhealthy dualisms, nonetheless, left a mark on certain Christian thinkers in the course of history and disfigured the Gospel."[5] John Paul II's TOB offers a definitive corrective to these disfigurements which have caused many Christians to grow up thinking of the physical world (especially their own bodies and sexuality) as something bad.

This is an ancient theological error called Manichaeism, and it couldn't be further from an authentic Christian perspective. In fact, it's a direct attack on Christianity at its deepest roots. *Everything* in the Christian faith hinges on the Incarnation, on the "Word made flesh." Ours is an *enfleshed* religion, and we must be very careful never to *un-flesh* it. It's always the enemy who wants to "deny Christ come in the flesh" (see 1 John 4:2–3).

If we're to rediscover who we really are, as John Paul II observed, it's necessary to contend with some "deep-seated habits" in our way of thinking that come from Manichaeism (see TOB 46:1). So let's take a closer look.

Mani (or Manichaeus), after whom this heresy is named, condemned the body and all things sexual because he believed that the material world was evil. Scripture, however, is very clear that everything God created is "very good" (see Genesis 1:31). This is a critical point to let sink in. Unwittingly, we often give evil far more weight than it deserves, as if the devil had created his own "evil world" to battle God's "good world." But the devil is a creature, not a creator. And this means the devil does not have his own clay. All he can do is take *God's* clay (which is always very good) and twist it, distort it. That's what evil *is*: the twisting or distortion of good. Redemption, therefore, involves the "untwisting" of what sin and evil have twisted so we can recover the true good.

In today's post–sexual revolution world, sin and evil have terribly twisted the meaning of sexuality and erotic love. But "the rejection of distortions of sexuality and eroticism should never lead us to a disparagement or neglect of sexuality and *eros* in themselves," insists Pope Francis.[6] That's a Manichaean approach. And if that's the approach we're taking, we haven't overcome the devil's lies. We've fallen right into his trap. His fundamental goal is always to split body and soul. Why? Well, there's a fancy theological word for the separation of body and soul. Perhaps you've heard of it: *death*. That's where Manichaeism, like all heresies, leads.

The true solution to pornographic distortions of the body is not the *rejection* of the body, but the *redemption* of the body—

the "untwisting" of what sin has twisted so we can recover the true glory, splendor, and inestimable value of the body. John Paul II summarized the critical distinction between the Manichaean and Christian approaches to the body as follows: If the Manichaean mentality places an "anti-value" on the body and sex, Christianity teaches that the body and sex "always remain a 'value not sufficiently appreciated'" (TOB, 45:3). In other words, if Manichaeism says "the body is bad," Christianity says "the body is so good we have yet to fathom it." The problem with our sex-saturated culture, then, is not that it overvalues the body and sex. The problem is that it has undervalued them; it has failed to see how incredibly valuable the body and sex really are.

We must say this loudly, clearly, and repeatedly until it sinks in and heals our wounds: Christianity does not *demonize* the body; Christianity *divinizes* the body! For Christ has raised the human body into the highest heights of the divine life! As the *Catechism* proclaims: "'The flesh is the hinge of salvation.' We believe in God who is creator of the flesh; we believe in the Word made flesh in order to redeem the flesh; we believe in the resurrection of the flesh, the fulfillment of both the creation and the redemption of the flesh" (*CCC*, 1015).

Bodily Suffering

Still, in the midst of rejoicing in this "ode to the flesh," how can we fail to acknowledge that, in this life, our bodiliness is often a source of great unhappiness and sometimes crushing suffering? Genetic defects, disease, sickness, injury, and a great many other physical maladies and misfortunes—not the least of which is the inevitable prospect of death—can tempt us to disdain our bodily existence. Sexual trauma, gender confusion, and disturbing, dark, and addictive sexual desires can cause us to feel ill at ease with or even loathe the fact that we are sexual beings.

In the face of such bitter trials and sufferings, how can we maintain that God is love and that our bodies are good? The following assertion of John Paul II offers much food for thought in this regard: "If the agony on the cross had not happened the truth that God is love would have been unfounded."[7] God does not turn a deaf ear to our cries. Quite the contrary, he enters into them, experiencing them himself in his passion and death, and, through his Resurrection, he transforms our sorrows into joy. Along the same lines we can add that if the Resurrection had not happened, the truth that the body is good would be unfounded. In fact, as St. Paul insists, if Christ has not been raised, our faith is futile (see 1 Corinthians 15:17). But if God has truly come in the flesh, if he has suffered, died, been buried, and risen again, then, united with Christ, all our wounds, maladies, and misfortunes can become something redemptive—for us and for others.

Learning and embracing the theology of our bodies takes us straight into the mystery of Christ's suffering body—always with the blessed assurance that our suffering leads to untold glory in the resurrection of our bodies. In fact, our sufferings *are* Christ's sufferings, for it was our sufferings that he endured. Whatever it is that we might suffer, we are "always carrying in the body the death of Jesus, so that the life of Jesus may also be manifested in our bodies" (2 Corinthians 4:10).

This is the story our bodies tell—the story of Christ's death and resurrection. This is what makes our bodies not only biological but theological. This is what makes our bodies sacramental.

The Sacramentality of the Body

In light of the mystery of the Incarnation, the Catholic faith has always recognized that matter matters. Catholicism is a very fleshy, sensual religion, much more so than some misguided forms of piety might wish it to be. Our most intimate encounters with God come through our bodily senses and the "stuff" of the material world: through bathing the body with water (baptism); anointing the body with oil (baptism, confirmation, holy orders, anointing of the sick); eating and drinking the Body and Blood of Christ (the Eucharist); the laying on of hands (holy orders, anointing of the sick); confessing with our lips to another body (penance); and the unbreakable joining of man and woman in "one flesh" (marriage).

How can we describe the "great mystery" of the sacraments? They are the physical means through which we encounter God's spiritual treasures. In the sacraments, spirit and matter "kiss." Heaven and earth embrace in a marriage that will never end.

The human body itself is in some sense a "sacrament." This is a broader and more ancient use of the word than we may be used to. Rather than referring to the seven signs of grace that Christ instituted, when John Paul II speaks of the body as a sacrament, he means it is a sign that somehow makes visible the invisible mystery of God.

We cannot see God. As we said above, God is pure spirit. And yet, St. John the Evangelist tells us that God's life was "made visible." Speaking of "the Word of life," the mystery "which was from the beginning," John claimed that he and his companions had *seen* this mystery "with their eyes" and had touched it "with their hands" (see 1 John 1:1–2). Christianity is the religion of

God's self-disclosure. God wants to reveal himself to us. He wants to make his invisible, spiritual mystery visible and tangible to us so that we can "see" him and "touch" him. How does he do so?

God speaks to us in sign language, revealing himself through the veil of this physical world. Most everyone has experienced that deep sense of awe and wonder in beholding a starlit night or a radiant sunset or a beautiful flower. In these moments, whether we realize it or not, we are reading God's sign language, seeing God's goodness and beauty reflected in his creation. "The beauty of creation reflects the infinite beauty of the Creator" (*CCC*, 341).

And yet there's something more grand than any starlit night, sunset, or flower. There's something at the pinnacle of creation that God designed in order to speak his sign language more potently, more poignantly than anything else. What is it? "God created man in his own image, in the image of God he created him; male and female he created them. And God blessed them and said to them, 'Be fruitful and multiply'" (Genesis 1:27–28). To say "theology of the body" is, in fact, just another way of saying we're made in the image and likeness of God.

Precisely in our creation as male and female and in our call to fruitful communion, the human body becomes the greatest sign of the spiritual and the divine. And the more we learn how to read this sign, the more we enter into the "great mystery" of who God is and what his eternal plan is for the human race.

John Paul II's Thesis

This brings us to the thesis statement of John Paul II's TOB, the brush with which he paints his entire vision. It's an incredibly dense statement, but fear not; we'll spend the rest of the book unfolding it. Here it is:

> The body, in fact, and only the body, is capable of making visible what is invisible: the spiritual and divine. It has been created to transfer into the visible reality of the world the mystery hidden from eternity in God, and thus to be a sign of it. (TOB 19:4)

Let's begin with the first sentence. Think of your own experiences as a human being: Your body is not just a shell in which you dwell. Your body is not just *a* body. Your body is not just *any* body. Your body is *some*body—you! Through the profound unity of your body and your soul, your body *reveals* or makes visible the invisible reality of your spiritual soul. The "you" you are is not just a soul in a body. Your body is not something you have or own alongside yourself. Your body *is* you. Which is why if someone broke your jaw in a fit of rage, you wouldn't take him to court for property damage but for personal assault. What we do with our bodies, and what is done to our bodies, we do or have done to *ourselves*.

Once again, our bodies make visible what is invisible—the spiritual *and the divine*. It's from this perspective that John Paul II wants to study the human body—not merely as a biological organism, but as a *theology*, as a "study of God."

The body is not divine, of course. But it *is* the most powerful sign of the divine mystery in all creation. A sign is something that points us to a reality beyond itself and, in some way, makes that transcendent reality present to us. The divine mystery always remains infinitely "beyond"; it cannot be reduced to its sign. Yet the sign is indispensable in making visible the invisible mystery. As the *Catechism* says, "Man needs signs and symbols to communicate. . . . The same holds true for his relationship with God" (*CCC*, 1146).

Tragically, because of sin, the "body loses its character as a sign" (TOB 40:4)—not objectively, but rather subjectively. In other words, in itself, the body retains its character as a sign of the spiritual and divine, but we've been blinded to it. We can't readily see it. As a result, we tend to consider the human body merely as a physical "thing" entirely separated from the spiritual and the divine. And this is why the very expression "theology of the body" seems so odd to people today, even to Christians. It shouldn't, if we believe in the Incarnation. As John Paul II put it, "Through the fact that the Word of God became flesh, the body entered theology . . . through the main door" (TOB 23:4).

We must say it again (and again!): *Everything* in Christianity hinges on the Incarnation. God's mystery has been revealed in human flesh, rendering the human body a study of God, a *theology*. Theology of the body, therefore, is not merely the title of a series of papal talks on sex and marriage; theology of the body is the very logic of Christianity. For in "the body of Jesus 'we see our God made visible and so are caught up in love of the God we cannot see'" (*CCC*, 477).

The Divine Mystery

Several times already we have spoken of the divine mystery or the "mystery hidden in God from all eternity" (see Ephesians 3:9). What does this mean? In the Christian sense, "mystery" does not refer to some unsolvable puzzle. It refers to the innermost "secret" of God and to his eternal plan for humanity. These realities are so far beyond anything we can comprehend that all we can really utter is the word "mystery." And yet God's secret is knowable—not based on our ability to decipher some divine puzzle, but because God has made it known.

As the *Catechism* says, "God has revealed his innermost secret: God himself is an eternal exchange of love, Father, Son, and Holy Spirit, and he has destined us to share in that exchange" (CCC, 221). God is not a tyrant; God is not a slave driver; God is not merely a legislator or lawgiver; and he's certainly not an old man with a white beard waiting to strike us down whenever we fail. God is an "eternal exchange of love." He's an infinite communion of persons experiencing eternal love-bliss. And he created us for one reason: to share that eternal love and bliss with us.

This is what makes the gospel *good news*: There is a banquet of love that corresponds to the hungry cry of our hearts, and it is God's free gift to us! We needn't climb some high mountain to find it. We needn't cross the sea. The "great mystery" of God's love is very close to us, intimately part of us. Indeed, God inscribed an image of this "great mystery" in the very form of our bodies by making us male and female and calling the two to become one flesh.

The Spousal Analogy

Scripture uses many images to help us understand God's love. Each has its own valuable place. But, as John Paul II wrote, the gift of Christ's body on the cross gives "definitive prominence to the spousal meaning of God's love."[8] In fact, from beginning to end, in the mysteries of our creation, fall, and redemption, the Bible tells a nuptial, or marital, story.

It begins in Genesis with the marriage of the first man and woman, and it ends in Revelation with the marriage of Christ and the Church. Right in the middle of the Bible we find the erotic poetry of the Song of Songs. These bookends and this centerpiece provide the key for reading the whole biblical story. Indeed, we can summarize all of Sacred Scripture with five simple, yet astounding words: *God wants to marry us.*

For as a young man marries a virgin
So shall your Maker marry you;
And as the bridegroom rejoices over his bride,
So shall your God rejoice over you. (Isaiah 62:5)

Your breasts were formed and your hair had grown
You were naked and bare.
When I passed by you again and looked upon you,
Behold, you were at the age for love . . .
I entered into a covenant with you, says the Lord
And you became mine. (Ezekiel 16:7–8)

And I will betroth you to me forever;
I will betroth you to me in righteousness and in justice,
In steadfast love, and in mercy.
I will betroth you to me in faithfulness;
And you shall know the Lord. (Hosea 2:19)

God is inviting each of us, in a unique and unrepeatable way, to an unimagined intimacy with him, akin to the intimacy of spouses in one flesh. In fact, as Pope Francis observes, "The very word [used in Scripture to describe marital union] . . . 'to cleave' . . . is used to describe our union with God: 'My soul clings to you' (Psalm 63:8)."[9] Because of the supreme bliss of union with God, "a love lacking either pleasure or passion is insufficient to symbolize the union of the human heart with God: 'All the mystics have affirmed that supernatural love and heavenly love find the symbols which they seek in marital love.'"[10]

While we may need to work through some discomfort or fear here to reclaim the true sacredness, the true holiness of the imagery, the "scandalous" truth is that Scripture describes "God's passion for his people using boldly erotic images," as Pope Benedict XVI put it.[11] In his Lenten Message 2007 he declared: "Eros is part of God's very Heart: the Almighty awaits the 'yes' of his creatures as a young bridegroom that of his bride."

We are probably more familiar (and more comfortable) describing God's love as *agape*—the Greek word for sacrificial, self-giving love. Yet God's love "may certainly be called *eros*," asserts Benedict XVI. In Christ *eros* is "supremely ennobled . . . so purified as to become one with *agape*." Thus, the Bible has no qualms employing the erotic poetry of the Song of Songs as a description of "God's relation to man and man's relation to God." In this way, as Benedict XVI concludes, the Song of Songs became not only an expression of the intimacies of marital love, it also became "an expression of the essence of biblical faith: that man can indeed enter into union with God—his primordial aspiration."[12]

The Essence of Biblical Faith

Let's try to let that sink in: The Song of Songs, this unabashed celebration of erotic love, expresses the essence of biblical faith.

How so? The essence of biblical faith is that God came among us in the flesh not only to forgive our sins (as astounding as that gift is); he became "one flesh" with us so that we could share in his eternal exchange of love. In the first of his many sermons on the Song of Songs, St. Bernard of Clairvaux aptly describes marriage as "the sacrament of endless union with God." Revelation calls this endless union the "marriage of the Lamb" (Revelation 19:7).

But there's more. Remember that pithy rhyme we learned as children: "First comes love, then comes marriage, then comes the baby in the baby carriage"? We probably didn't realize that we were actually reciting some profound *theology*: theology *of the body*! Our bodies tell the story that God loves us, wants to marry us, and wants us to "conceive" eternal life within us. "What is happening here?" asks St. Bonaventure. When God fills us with his divine life, it is "nothing other than the heavenly Father by a divine seed, as it were, impregnating the soul and making it fruitful."[13]

For Christians, the idea of divine impregnation is not merely a metaphor. Representing all of us, a young Jewish woman named Mary once gave her "yes" to God's marriage proposal with such totality and fidelity that she literally conceived eternal life in her womb. In a hymn addressed to her, St. Augustine exclaims: "The Word becomes united with flesh, he makes his covenant with flesh, and your womb is the sacred bed on which this holy union of the Word with flesh is consummated."[14] Mary's virginity has always been understood by the Church as the sign of her betrothal to God. She is the "mystic bride of love eternal," as a traditional hymn has it. As such, Mary perfectly fulfills the spousal character of the human vocation in relation to God (see *CCC*, 505).

In turn, Mary fully illuminates the theology of a woman's body. In her, woman's body has literally become the dwelling place of the Most High God—heaven on earth! Every woman shares in some way in this incomparable dignity and calling. Every woman's body is a sign of heaven on earth. And, oh, how lovely is your dwelling place, Lord, mighty God (see Psalm 84:1). Continue unfolding this astounding mystery and it's not difficult to recognize that the theology of a man's body can be described as a call to enter the gates of heaven, to surrender himself there, to lay down his life there by pouring himself out utterly. In this way the man images the eternal outpouring, the eternal life-givingness of God as Father.

Can we even imagine a greater sacredness, a greater holiness, a greater goodness and glory ascribed to our maleness and femaleness, our sexuality? Oh, Lord, show us who we really are! Give us eyes to see so glorious a mystery revealed through our bodies and in the call of man and woman to become one flesh!

Penetrating the Essence of the Mystery

In the midst of unfolding the biblical analogy of spousal love, it's very important to understand the bounds within which we're using such language and imagery. Analogies, of course, always indicate both a similarity and an even more substantial dissimilarity. Without this recognition, there is a real danger of inferring too much about divine realities, based on human realities.

"It is obvious," writes John Paul II, "that the analogy of . . . human spousal love . . . cannot offer an adequate and complete understanding of . . . the divine mystery." God's "*mystery* remains *transcendent with respect to this analogy* as with respect to any other analogy." At the same time, however, John Paul II maintains that the spousal analogy allows a certain "penetration" into the very essence of the mystery (see TOB 95b:1). And no biblical author reaches more deeply into this essence than St. Paul in his letter to the Ephesians.

Quoting directly from Genesis, Paul states: "'For this reason a man shall leave his father and mother and be joined to his wife, and the two shall become one flesh.'" Then, linking the original marriage with the ultimate marriage, he adds: "This is a great mystery, and I mean in reference to Christ and the Church" (Ephesians 5:31–32).

We can hardly overstate the importance of this passage for John Paul II and the whole theological tradition of the Church. He calls it the "summa" ("sum total") of Christian teaching about who God is and who we are.[15] He says this passage contains the "crowning" of all the themes in Sacred Scripture and expresses the "central reality" of the whole of divine revelation (see TOB 87:3). The mystery spoken of in this passage "is *'great' indeed*," he says. "It is what God . . . wishes above all to transmit to mankind in his Word." Thus, "one can say that [this] passage . . . 'reveals— in a particular way—*man to man himself* and makes *his supreme vocation* clear' (GS, 22)" (TOB 87:6; 93:2).

So what is this "supreme vocation" we have as human beings that Ephesians 5 makes clear? Stammering for words to describe the ineffable, the mystics call it "nuptial union" . . . *with God.*[16] Christ is the new Adam who left his Father in heaven. He also left the home of his mother on earth. Why? To mount "the marriage bed of the cross," as St. Augustine had it, unite himself with the

Church, symbolized by "the woman" at the foot of the cross, and consummate the union forever. Archbishop Fulton Sheen elaborates:

> Now we've always thought, and rightly so, of Christ the Son on the cross and the mother beneath him. But that's not the complete picture. That's not the deep understanding. Who is our Lord on the cross? He's the new Adam. Where's the new Eve? At the foot of the cross. . . . If Eve became the mother of the living in the natural order, is not this woman at the foot of the cross to become another mother? [How does this spiritual motherhood happen?] . . . As St. Augustine puts it, and here I am quoting him verbatim, ". . . As it were, the blood and water that came from the side of Christ was the spiritual seminal fluid." And so from these nuptials "Woman, there's your son" this is the beginning of the Church.[17]

"On the Cross, God's eros for us is made manifest," proclaims Pope Benedict XVI. "Eros is indeed . . . that force which 'does not allow the lover to remain in himself but moves him to become one with the beloved.' Is there more 'mad eros' . . . than that which led the Son of God to make himself one with us even to the point of suffering as his own the consequences of our offenses?" he asks.[18]

The more we allow the brilliant rays of Christ's "mad eros" to illuminate our vision, the more we come to understand, as the *Catechism* observes, how the "entire Christian life bears the mark of the spousal love of Christ and the Church. Already Baptism, the entry into the People of God, is a nuptial mystery" (*CCC*, 1617). Here "the 'imperishable seed' of the Word of God produces its life-giving effect" (*CCC*, 1228). The "imperishable seed" is given by Christ as Bridegroom and received by the Church as Bride. And through these glorious, virginal nuptials, the Church brings forth sons and daughters "to a new and immortal life" (*CCC*, 507).

Still, as glorious as baptism is, it's only our entry into the Christian life, not its summit. Baptism opens the way to the sacrament of sacraments, the mystery of mysteries; baptism "is so to speak the nuptial bath which precedes the wedding feast, the Eucharist" (*CCC*, 1617).

The Summit of the Spousal Analogy

In the Eucharist, "Christ is united with his 'body' as the bridegroom with the bride," John Paul II tells us. As such, the Eucharist illuminates with supernatural brilliance "the relationship between man and woman, between what is 'feminine' and what is 'masculine.'"[19] It is in the Eucharist that the meaning of life, love, sex, gender, and marriage is fully revealed! How so?

There is such a strong temptation to disincarnate and, thus, neuter our faith that we're often oblivious to the profound significance of the fact that there is a *man* on the cross and a *woman* at the foot of the cross. It can't be the other way around. In the spousal analogy, God is always the Bridegroom and humanity is always the Bride. Why? Because humanity is first receptive to the love of God: "In this is love, not that we loved God, but that he first loved us" (1 John 4:10). The woman's body primarily tells the story of *receiving* divine love while the man's body primarily tells the story of *offering* that love, of pouring it out.

The more we press in to this divine love story, the more we realize why only a man can be an ordained priest: It's the bridegroom who gives the seed or inseminates; it's the bride who receives the seed within and conceives new life. This is why a man trains to be a priest in the *seminary* and, once ordained, is called *Father*. A woman cannot be ordained a priest because she is not ordained by God to be a father; she is ordained by God to be a mother. This is where the sexual difference matters—in the call to holy communion and generation. If a woman were to attempt to confer the Eucharist, the relationship would be bride to bride. There would be no possibility of Holy Communion and no possibility of generating new life.

Of course, a world that insists that two women can marry will also insist that a woman can be a priest, but both ideas come from the same failure to recognize the essential meaning of the sexual difference. Since grace builds on nature, when we're confused about the natural reality, we're also confused about the supernatural reality: "If I have told you earthly things and you do not believe," asks Jesus, "how can you believe if I tell you heavenly things?" (John 3:12).

The more deeply we enter into the "great mystery" of Ephesians 5, the more we will see how and why the sexual difference is just as important to the Holy Communion of the Eucharist as it is to the holy communion of marriage. In fact, as John Paul II teaches, we cannot understand one without the other. Perhaps the following story will illuminate what he means.

I never met my father-in-law. He died when my wife was a girl, but I admire him tremendously because of the intuition he had as a brand-new husband. At Mass the day after his wedding, having consummated his marriage the night before, he was in tears as he came back to the pew after receiving the Eucharist.

When his new bride inquired, he said, "For the first time in my life I understood the meaning of those words, 'This is my body given for you.'"

Make no mistake: When all the smoke is cleared and all the distortions are untwisted, the deepest meaning and purpose of human sexuality is to point us to the Eucharist, the "marriage supper of the Lamb" (Revelation 19:9). And this is precisely why questions of sex, gender, and marriage place us right in the center of "the situation in which *the powers of good and evil fight against each other*" (TOB 115:2).

The Body and the Spiritual Battle

If God created the body and sexual union to proclaim his own eternal mystery of love, why do we not typically see and experience them in this profound way? For example, when you hear the word "sex," what generally comes to mind? Is it the great mystery of Ephesians 5 . . . or is it something, shall we say, a little less sacred than that? Remember, it's because of sin that the "body loses its character as a sign" of the divine mystery (see TOB 40:4).

Ponder this for a moment: If the union of the sexes is the main sign in this world of our call to union with God, and if there is an enemy who wants to separate us from God, where do you think he's going to aim his most potent arrows? If we want to know what is most sacred in this world, all we need do is look for what is most violently profaned.

We live in a world of chaotic, widespread gender confusion, a world that seems intent on erasing the essential meaning of the sexual difference from the individual and collective consciousness. Where does this confusion ultimately come from? What spiritual forces might be instigating it and why? Professor Stanislaw Grygiel of the John Paul II Institute for Studies on Marriage and Family expressed it this way:

> If we don't live the sexual differences correctly that distinguish men and women and call them to unite, we will not be capable of understanding the difference that distinguishes Man and God, and constitutes a primordial call to union. Thus, we may fall into the despair of a life separated from others and from the Other, that is, God.[20]

It is sobering in the utmost to think that all the sexual confusion in our world today might be the unfolding of a diabolic plot to separate us from one another and from God. This much is certain from Paul's letter to the Ephesians: The battle for man's soul is fought over the truth of his body. It's no mere coincidence that Paul follows his presentation of the ultimate meaning of gender, sex, and marriage in Ephesians 5 with his call to spiritual warfare in Ephesians 6. These issues place us "at the center of the great struggle between good and evil, between life and death, between love and all that is opposed to love."[21] That's why the first thing we must do to win this battle is "gird [our] loins with the truth" (Ephesians 6:14).

The TOB is John Paul II's clarion call for all men and women to do just that—to gird their loins with the truth that will set them free to love; the truth that will reunite men and women with one another in the image of God and, thus, reunite them with God himself.

The Foundation of Ethics and Culture

The stakes are incredibly high in the cultural debates about the meaning of gender, sex, and marriage—and not only in the spiritual or religious realm. Confusion about the meaning of sexuality leads to the "moral disorder that deforms . . . the functioning of *social, economic* and even cultural *life*" (TOB 51, note 61).

The communion of man and woman is "the deepest substratum [or foundation] of human ethics and culture" (TOB 45:3). In short, as our understanding of gender and sex go, so goes marriage; as marriage goes, so goes the family. And because the family is the fundamental cell of society, as the family goes, so goes the world. Hence, confusion about sexual morality, as John Paul II wrote in his pre-papal book *Love and Responsibility*, "involves a danger perhaps greater than is generally realized: the danger of confusing the basic and fundamental human tendencies, the main paths of human existence."[22]

Think how intertwined sex is with the very reality of human existence. You simply would not exist without the sexual union of your parents . . . and their parents . . . and their parents. Your existence depends on a chain of thousands upon thousands of indispensable sexual unions that link to the beginning of human history. Go back any number of generations in your family tree and remove (or sterilize) just one sexual union in your lineage, and you would not exist. Nor would anyone else who descended from that point on the family tree. The world would be a different place.

When we tinker with God's plan for sex, we are tinkering with the cosmic stream of human existence. The human race—its very existence and its proper balance—is literally determined by who is having sex with whom, and in what manner. When sexual union is oriented toward love and life, it builds families and, in turn, cultures that live the truth of love and life. When it is oriented against love and life, the sexual act breeds death— what John Paul II grimly, yet accurately, described as a "culture of death."

The Interconnection of Sex and the Whole of Life

A "culture of death" is a culture that separates body and soul (remember, that's what death *is*). In turn, it cannot recognize the body as a sign of anything spiritual, let alone divine. It can't recognize the "great mystery" of married love and procreation. Sex, instead, gets reduced merely to the pursuit of pleasure.

Sexual pleasure is a great blessing and gift from God, of course. But it is meant to be the fruit of loving as he loves, not an end in itself. When pleasure becomes the main goal of sex, society becomes utilitarian. You're valued if you're useful. And, in this case, you're useful if you stimulate my lusts. If you don't, or if you get in the way of my pleasure, you will be ignored, discarded, maybe even exterminated. When pleasure is the main goal of sex, people become the means and babies become the obstacle. So we take our pleasure and we kill our offspring.

This is not a dire prediction of an apocalyptic future. *This is the culture we live in now*—a culture of death. John Paul II summarized the situation very soberly: "It is an illusion to think we can build a true culture of human life if we do not . . . accept and experience sexuality and love and the whole of life according to their true meaning and their close interconnection."[23] This is precisely why

John Paul II gave us the TOB: to help us accept and experience sexuality and love and the whole of life according to their true meaning and their close interconnection and, in that way, build a true culture of human life from the ground up.

John Paul II's Approach

One of the main reasons John Paul II's TOB resonates so deeply with people is the philosophical approach that undergirds it. In contrast to more conventional philosophical approaches that focus on objective categories and abstract concepts, John Paul II focuses on the familiar realm of subjective human experiences. He believes that if what the Church teaches is objectively true, then human experience—subjective as it is—should offer confirmation of that truth. Knowing that the Church's message "is in harmony with the most secret desires of the human heart" (CCC, 2126), John Paul II does not need to nor does he attempt to force assent to his proposals. Rather, he invites men and women to reflect honestly on their own experience of life to see if it confirms his proposals.

Those who have been turned off by judgmental moralizers will find this approach delightfully refreshing. John Paul II imposes nothing and wags a finger at no one. He simply reflects lovingly on God's Word and on human experience in order to demonstrate the profound harmony between them. Then, with utmost respect for our freedom, he invites us to embrace our own dignity. It doesn't matter how often we have settled for something less. This is a message of sexual healing and redemption, not condemnation.

With this compassionate and merciful approach—the Gospel approach—John Paul II shifts the discussion about sex from *legalism* to *liberty*. The legalist asks, "How far can I go before

I break the law?" Instead, John Paul II asks, "What is the truth about sex that sets me free to love?" To answer that question, we must ask why God made us male and female in the first place. These are questions that plunge us into the deepest truth of what it means to be human. Indeed, the "fundamental fact" of human existence "is that God 'created [us] male and female'" (TOB 18:4).

What John Paul II's TOB is primarily seeking to provide, then, is the full truth of what it means to be human—or, as he puts it, a "total vision of man." To discover this total vision, we must turn to Christ, the one who alone "fully reveals man to himself and makes his supreme calling clear."[24] This line from the Second Vatican Council was John Paul II's anthem: Christ, precisely by taking on flesh, fully reveals what it means to be human. And so Part I of John Paul II's TOB is called "The Words of Christ" and is based on three key words of Jesus—three appeals he makes— that paint a three-paneled picture of where we've come from (our origin), where we are now (our history), and where we're headed (our destiny):

1. *Christ Appeals to the "Beginning"*: based on Jesus' discussion with the Pharisees about God's plan for marriage "in the beginning" (see Matthew 19:3–9).

2. *Christ Appeals to the Human Heart*: based on Jesus' words in the Sermon on the Mount regarding adultery committed "in the heart" (see Matthew 5:27–28).

3. *Christ Appeals to the Resurrection*: based on Christ's statement to the Sadducees that in the resurrection men and women no longer marry (see Matthew 22: 23–33).

For our purposes, I've titled the corresponding chapters in this book as follows: "The Creation of the Body," "The Redemption of the Body," and "The Resurrection of the Body." Only in light of these three stages of the human drama can we understand both *what it means to be human* and, based on that, *how to live our lives in a way that brings true happiness*.

Revelation teaches that there are essentially two ways of living the truth of our sexuality in its totality: celibacy and marriage.[25] So, before he concludes Part I of the TOB, John Paul II reflects on Christ's words about those who choose to forgo marriage for the sake of the kingdom of heaven, demonstrating Christian celibacy to be a fully human—and, yes, fully sexual—vocation. If that seems like a contradiction, it won't by the time you've finished reading chapter five of this book.

Part II of the TOB is called "The Sacrament." Here John Paul II reflects on marriage both as a *divine gift* and a *human sign* of divine love. Chapters six and seven of this book are titled accordingly. Only in light of these two dimensions of the sacrament of marriage are we capable of understanding the true language of sexual love. And that's where John Paul II takes us in the final section of his TOB: to a winning explanation of how the Christian sexual ethic flows very naturally from a total vision of what it means to be human. For our purposes, I've called that chapter "Theology in the Bedroom."

Having set the stage by exploring what the TOB is, we're now ready to dive in to the content of John Paul II's teaching itself.

FOR REFLECTION

1. If God created the body and sexual union to express the eternal mystery of his own divine love, why do we not typically see and experience them in this profound way? Why is there so much confusion about the meaning of the body and of sex today?

2. Describe in your own words what St. John Paul II meant by the "culture of death." What examples of this culture do you observe around you?

3. How might understanding the truth about sexuality transform the way you approach relationships with the opposite sex?

Dear Lord, as we explore the deep truths that St. John Paul II wrote about in his Theology of the Body, open our eyes to see the plan for human love that you have written in our bodies.

TWO

The Creation of the Body

This is the body: a witness . . . to Love.
—St. John Paul II

In the last few years, I've taken up backpacking with my sons. Venturing off into God's creation for several days, away from everything, with all you need strapped to your back; the smell of the woods; the crystal clear streams, waterfalls, and swimming holes; the views from the summit after a long climb; cooking breakfast over the fire—I love it! Getting eaten alive by mosquitos; getting soaked to the bone by rain; having no choice but to plod forward when your back is killing you, your legs want to give out, and each step causes your blisters to scream—I hate it! In fact, the best thing about a backpacking trip is getting to the car you left behind five days and fifty miles earlier. So why leave the car in the first place? Because *it's all about the journey*.

After observing that the Gospels are filled with stories of Jesus teaching his disciples as they walked, Pope Francis stated, "This is important. Jesus did not come to teach a philosophy, an ideology, but rather a 'way,' a journey to be undertaken with him, and we learn the way as we go, by walking."[26] Backpacking, for me, has become a "sacrament" of that journey: an outward sign of an inner reality. In both the joys and the trials, it gives visceral, bodily expression to what I experience interiorly on the journey of following Christ. Pope Benedict XVI put words to the "outer" and "inner" realities of the Christian journey in a homily on the Three Wise Men:

> These men who set out toward the unknown were . . . men with a restless heart; men driven by a restless quest for God. . . . They wanted to know how we succeed in being human. . . . They wanted to understand the truth about God and the world. Their outward pilgrimage was an expression of their inward journey, the inner pilgrimage of their hearts . . .
>
> Human beings have an innate restlessness for God, but this restlessness is a participation in God's own restlessness for us. . . . Faith draws us into a state of being seized by the restlessness of God and it makes us pilgrims who are on an inner journey . . .
>
> [To make their journey, the Wise Men had to be], above all, men of courage, the courage and humility born of faith. Courage was needed to grasp the meaning of the star as a sign, and to set out, to go forth— toward the unknown, the uncertain, on paths filled with hidden dangers . . . The Wise Men [faced these dangers], followed the star, and thus came to Jesus, to the great light that enlightens everyone.[27] (January 6, 2013)

As we learned in the previous chapter, everything in creation— be it a star or a flower—is a sign that, if followed, leads to God.

But the greatest of these signs in all creation is the human body in its masculinity and femininity. Much like the Wise Men, as we venture into the content of St. John Paul II's TOB, we will need courage to grasp the meaning of the body as a sign and to follow that sign into the unknown, on paths filled with hidden dangers.

To go where this great sign leads means a long journey. In fact, in this life, it's never ending. It will be exhilarating and, at times, very difficult. There will be moments when your back is killing you, your legs want to give out, and each step causes your blisters to scream. *Keep going!* Keep putting one foot in front of the other, and, like the Wise Men in the Gospel, your journey will lead you to an encounter with the "great mystery" that is Christ; and through that encounter, you will come to understand, also like the Wise Men, "the truth about God and the world" and how to "succeed in being human." Understanding the body as a great sign that leads us to this truth and this success starts with Christ's appeal to "the beginning."

Christ Appeals to the Beginning

When some Pharisees questioned Jesus about the meaning of marriage, Jesus responded, "Have you not read that he who made them from the beginning made them male and female . . . ?" (Matthew 19:4).

If we need proof of the pertinence of these words today, look no further than the fact that Facebook recently listed over fifty gender options to choose from when filling out a personal profile. After complaints that terms such as "intersex," "cisgender," "gender fluid," "gender noncomforming," "gender variant," "neutrois," "non-binary," "pangender," "two-spirit," and multiple other variations on these themes were too limiting, the site added a "free-form field" in which people can now "customize" their gender identity. "We recognize that some people face challenges sharing their true gender identity with others," said Facebook's diversity team in a statement, "and this setting gives people the ability to express themselves in an authentic way."

What does it mean—really—to speak of "true gender identity" and to express it "in an authentic way"? According to Christ, the answers can only be found by returning to God's original purpose for making us male and female before the confusion of sin obscured it. Only by doing so can we save the term "gender" from the insanity of a world untethered from reality.

The root *gen*—from which we get words like generous, generate, genesis, genetics, genealogy, progeny, gender, and genitals—means to produce or give birth to. A person's *gen*-der, therefore, is based on the manner in which that person is designed to *gen*-erate new life. Contrary to widespread secular insistence, a person's gender is not a malleable social construct. Rather, a person's gender is determined by the kind of genitals he or she has. While the sexual and feminist revolutions of the twentieth century were right to challenge certain roles conventionally limited to one or the other gender, there are two roles—one belonging only to men and the other only to women—that are inalterable and absolutely indispensable for the survival of the human race: fatherhood and motherhood. When we understand the gender-genitals-generation link, we also understand why a de-gendered society is bound to de-generate. Indeed, failing to honor the God-given meaning of gender places the future of the human race in peril.

Pope Francis observed that today "various forms of an ideology of gender . . . envisage a society without sexual differences, thereby eliminating the anthropological basis of the family. This ideology . . . promote[s] a personal identity and emotional intimacy radically separated from the biological difference between male and female. Consequently, human identity becomes the choice of the individual, one that can also change over time. . . . It is one thing to be understanding of human weakness and the complexities of life," says Francis, "and another to accept ideologies that attempt to sunder what are inseparable aspects of reality." We "are called to protect our humanity," he insists, "and this means, in the first place, accepting it and respecting it as it was created [by God]."[28] Christ calls us to this respect by reminding us of "the beginning" when God created us as male and female (see Matthew 19:4).

Inevitably, the question arises in this context about those people born with ambiguous genitalia. While acknowledging that this is indeed a painful reality of our fallen world, John Paul II nonetheless observes that everyone "belongs from birth to one of the two sexes. This fact is not contradicted by [those rare cases of] hermaphroditism—any more than any other sickness or deformity militates against the fact that there is such a thing as human nature."[29] In other words, the anomaly doesn't alter the norm. The hope for those who suffer with this anomaly, and for all those with gender confusion of any kind, lies not in science to "assign" a new gender, but in Christ to restore the original order of our humanity through the gift of redemption.

Whatever number of "genders identities" the modern world

may claim exists, Christ's teaching is definitive: "He who made them from the beginning made them male and female." Then, quoting from Genesis, he adds, "'For this reason a man shall leave his father and mother and be joined to his wife, and the two shall become one flesh.' So they are no longer two but one flesh. What therefore God has joined together"—the two genders, through their complementary genitals, for the sake of generation—"let not man put asunder" (Matthew 19:4–6).

From the Beginning It Was Not So

Shocked by Jesus' insistence on the indissolubility of marriage, the Pharisees retorted, "Why then did Moses command one to give a certificate of divorce, and to put her away?" In response, Christ appealed to the beginning yet again: "For your hardness of heart Moses allowed you to divorce your wives, but from the beginning it was not so" (Matthew 19:8).

Jesus does not accept the normalization of our fallen humanity. In effect, he is saying something like this: "You think all the tension, conflict, and heartache in the male-female relationship is normal? This is not normal. This is not the way God created it to be. Something has gone terribly wrong." As the *Catechism* expresses it, the disorder we notice so painfully in the male-female relationship "does not stem from the *nature* of man and woman, nor from the nature of their relations, but from *sin*. As a break with God, the first sin had for its consequence the rupture of the original communion between man and woman" (CCC, 1607).

Because of the effects of sin, it's as if we're all driving around town in cars with flat tires. The rubber is shredding off the rims;

the rims are getting dented up; and we think it's all normal. After all, everyone's tires look this way. Jesus is saying to the Pharisees (and to all of us), "In the beginning, they had air in their tires." At the same time—and this is the good news!—Christ is injecting his listeners with hope . . . hope of restoration . . . hope of healing . . . hope of redemption. For "Jesus came to restore creation to the purity of its origins" (CCC, 2336).

As we look at John Paul II's reflections on the creation texts, we will probably realize at a new level just how far we are from "the beginning." But do not despair! Christ came into the world not to condemn those with flat tires. He came into the world to reinflate our flat tires. While we cannot actually return to the state of innocence, by God's grace we can receive his original plan for our sexuality and live it (see CCC, 1615). This is good news!

Original Human Experiences

Recall that John Paul II's approach is to reflect on familiar human experiences. This affords a delightfully refreshing look at the creation stories. We, of course, do not have any direct experience of how the first man and woman lived and embraced their bodies and sexuality in the state of original innocence. Nonetheless, John Paul II maintains that an "echo" of the beginning exists within each of us. The original human experiences, he says, "are always at the root of every human experience . . . Indeed, they are so interwoven with the ordinary things of life that we generally do not realize their extraordinary character" (TOB 11:1).

We approach these experiences through "the symbolism of biblical language" (CCC, 375). Symbolism is the most apt way to convey deep spiritual truths, which is what Genesis seeks to do.

We need not get hung up on the modern assertion that science has "disproved" the creation stories in Genesis. The creation stories were never meant to be scientific accounts of the origin of the world (the scientific method wasn't even developed until the late Middle Ages). Scientific knowledge is certainly valuable as far is it goes, but it cannot tell us the spiritual *meaning* of our existence. For this, the divinely inspired authors of Scripture employed the symbolism with which we are familiar.

Here's an analogy. Consider the difference for a woman when her optometrist looks in her eyes and when her husband or boyfriend does so. The scientist is looking at her cornea and records the scientific facts. The lover is looking at her soul and proclaims something more poetic and inspired (we hope). Does the scientist "disprove" the lover? No. These are simply two perspectives on the same reality. The author of Genesis was not a scientist but a lover, inspired by God to proclaim the spiritual mysteries at the origin of the world and of mankind. We must keep this in mind as we examine the creation stories.

According to John Paul II, three experiences in particular define the human person in the state of innocence: *solitude, unity*, and *nakedness*. Much ink can be spilled unpacking his profound reflections on these experiences (see my book *Theology of the Body Explained*). Here, of course, I am only presenting a basic sketch. As I do, see if you do not find an "echo" of these experiences in your own heart.

Original Solitude

"Then the Lord God said, 'It is not good that the man should be alone; I will make him a helper fit for him'" (Genesis 2:18). The most obvious meaning of this "solitude" is that the man is alone without the woman. But John Paul II mines a deeper meaning from this verse. This creation account doesn't even distinguish between male and female until after Adam's "deep sleep." Here Adam represents all of us—men and women (*adam* in Hebrew means "man" in the generic sense). Man is "alone" because he is the only bodily creature made in God's image and likeness. In other words, man is "alone" in the visible world as a *person*.

When Adam names the animals, he also discovers his own "name," his own identity. He was looking for a "helper," but he didn't find one among the animals (see Genesis 2:20). Adam *differs* from the animals, and "person" is the word we've coined to make the distinction. What does the human *person* have that the animals don't? In a word, freedom. Adam is not determined by bodily instinct. He is created from "the dust" like the animals (he is bodily), but he also has the "breath of life" inspiring his body (see Genesis 2:7). An inspired body is not just *a* body but *some*body. A *person* can choose what to do with his or her body. Mere dust cannot.

In this freedom, Adam experiences himself as a *self*. He is more than an "object" in the world; he is also a "subject." He has an inner world or an inner life. It's impossible to speak of the inner life of a squirrel or a chicken. It's precisely this inner life that the words *subject* and *person* capture. Despite some modern propaganda to the contrary, we know intuitively that chickens are not "people, too." We owe special respect to all of God's creatures (see *CCC*, 2415–18), yet no other bodily creature shares the dignity of being created in God's image.

Why was Adam endowed with freedom? Because Adam was called to love, and without freedom, love is impossible. In his solitude, Adam realizes that love is his origin, his vocation, and his destiny. He realizes that, unlike the animals, he is invited to enter a covenant of love with God himself. The Creator wants to marry his creature; God is "a lover with all the passion of a true love."[30] It's this relationship of love with God that defines Adam's solitude more than anything else. Tasting this love, he also longs with all his being to share a covenant of love with another person like himself. This is why it is "not good that the man should be alone."

In his solitude, therefore, Adam has already discovered his twofold vocation: love of God and love of neighbor (see Mark 12:29–31). He has also discovered his capacity to negate this vocation. God *invites* Adam to love; he never forces him because *forced* love is not love at all. Adam can say "yes" to God's invitation, or he can say "no." And this fundamental choice is expressed and realized *in his body*. Solitude—the first discovery of personhood and freedom—is something spiritual, but it is experienced bodily. As John Paul II says, the "body expresses the person" (TOB 7:2). We can also say, the body expresses the freedom of the person, or at least it's meant to.

If we reclaim this terribly abused phrase and restore its authentic meaning, we can recognize that God is entirely "pro-choice"—in other words, he is entirely "for" our freedom since he gave us freedom in the first place. But some choices negate our vocation to love. Some choices can *never* bring happiness. We *are* "free" in a sense to "do whatever we want with our bodies." However, we are not free to determine whether what we do with our bodies is good or evil. As Adam learned, this is a tree (the "tree of the knowledge of good and evil") from which he cannot eat, lest he die (see Genesis 2:16–17). Therefore, human freedom is fully realized not by inventing good and evil, but by choosing properly between them.

All of these insights are contained in the experience of Adam's solitude. Freedom is given for love. It's intended to establish communion and bestow life. Cut off from love, self-indulgence masquerades as "freedom" and leads to rupture and death. What kind of freedom do we want? As Genesis tells us, it's our *choice*.

Original Unity

After Adam named all the animals without finding a person among them, we can imagine his sentiment upon seeing the woman. Adam's cry, "This at last is bone of my bones and flesh of my flesh!" (Genesis 2:23), expresses absolute wonder and fascination.

Notice the bodily focus. Adam is fascinated with *her body* because, as John Paul II points out, this "at last" is a body that expresses a person. All the animals he named were bodies, but not persons. We lose this in English, but for the Jews, "flesh" and "bones" signified the whole human being. Hence, woman's creation from one of Adam's bones (see Genesis 2:21–22) is a figurative way of expressing that both men and women share the same humanity. Both are persons made in God's image. Both are alone in the world in the sense that they are both *different* from the animals (original solitude); both are called to live in a covenant of love. "Therefore a man leaves his father and his mother and cleaves to his wife, and they become one flesh" (Genesis 2:24).

This experience of *unity* overcomes man's *solitude*, in the sense of being alone without the "other." But it affirms everything about human solitude, in the sense that man and woman are both persons different from the animals. While it functions much the same biologically, the human union in one flesh is worlds apart from the copulation of animals. What's the difference? In God's original design, man and woman's sexual desires were not driven by instinct as with the animals. They flowed precisely from the freedom to love in the image of God. In other words, eros expressed agape. This is what makes human sexuality not only a biological reality but a theological reality.

The Communion of Persons

Becoming one flesh, therefore, is not only the joining of two bodies (as with animals), but also a "'sacramental' expression which corresponds to the communion of persons" (TOB 31:2). Animals are able to mate, but they're not able to enter "communion." Only *persons* are capable of the "gift of self" that establishes a common-union. The term "communion of persons," therefore, is very important in John Paul II's explanation of the meaning of marriage and sexual union.

Describing the one-flesh union as a sacramental expression takes us back to our earlier discussion of the sacramentality of the human body. The human body makes visible the invisible mystery of God, who himself is an *eternal* communion of persons. Within the Trinity, the Father eternally "begets" the Son by *giving himself* to and for the Son. In turn, the Son (the "beloved of the Father") eternally receives the love of the Father and eternally gives himself back to the Father. The love they share *is* the Holy Spirit, who, as we say in the Nicene Creed, "proceeds from the Father and the Son."

In turn, the function of man and woman being made in the image of God "is that of mirroring the one who is the model, of reproducing its own prototype" (TOB 9:3). And here, John Paul II presents an important and rather dramatic development in Catholic thinking. Traditionally, theologians have said we image God as individuals, through our rational souls. This is certainly true. But John Paul II takes it a step further. Although he never lines up husband, wife, and offspring with specific Persons of the Trinity, he does maintain that man images God "not only through his own humanity, but also through the communion of persons which man and woman form right from the beginning." And, rather poetically, he observes that on "all this, right from the beginning, the blessing of fruitfulness descended" (TOB 9:3).

This "blessing of fruitfulness" that descends from "the Lord, the giver of life" (Nicene Creed) reveals the mystery of a third who proceeds from them both. "Seen this way the couple's fruitful relationship becomes an image for understanding and describing the mystery of God himself."[31] In other words, sexual love as God designed it is a theology lesson; it's an icon or earthly image of the inner life of the Trinity. Even more, "the Trinity is present in the temple of marital communion," as Pope Francis put it.[32] Can we possibly imagine a more exalted vision of human sexuality than this? John Paul II even says that this understanding of the image of God "constitutes, perhaps, the deepest theological aspect of everything one can say about man" (TOB 9:3). It takes us "within the very bone marrow" of the theology of the body, which "becomes in some way also a theology of sex, or rather a theology of masculinity and femininity" (TOB 9:5).

Pope Francis, building on the insights of his predecessor, observed that the

> sexual difference is present in many forms of life, in the long ladder of living things. But only in man and woman does it bear within it the image and likeness of God . . . This tells us that not only is man taken by himself the image of God, that not only woman taken by herself is the image of God, but also man and woman, as a couple, are the image of God. The difference between man and woman is . . . for communion and procreation, always in the image and likeness of God.[33]

Of course, none of this means that God is sexual. The mystery of love and generation in the Trinity is infinitely beyond that of human love and generation. The *Catechism* states this clearly:

> In no way is God in man's image. He is neither man nor woman. God is pure spirit in which there is no place for the difference between the sexes. But the respective "perfections" of man and woman reflect something of the infinite perfection of God. (*CCC*, 370; see also *CCC*, 42, 239)

It's that "something" that John Paul II is pressing into and unfolding for us at great length in his TOB. The earthly image may pale in comparison to the divine reality. Nonetheless, God created us as male and female and called us to communion as the original and fundamental revelation of his own mystery in the created world. This is what John Paul II means when he describes marriage as the "primordial sacrament" (see TOB 96).

"In this entire world there is not a more perfect, more complete image of God," he says. "There is no other human reality which corresponds more, humanly speaking, to that divine mystery."[34]

Original Nakedness

Having discussed the original experiences of *solitude* and *unity*, we are ready to explore the third original experience—*nakedness*.

After the words describing their unity in one flesh, we read that "the man and his wife were both naked, and were not ashamed" (Genesis 2:25). Of all the passages in the creation stories, John Paul II boldly asserts that this one is "precisely the key" for understanding God's original plan for human life. In short, if we do not understand the meaning of original nakedness, we do not understand the meaning of our creation as male and female; we do not understand ourselves and the meaning of life.

But how can we understand nakedness without shame when we, having inherited the "fig leaves," have no direct experience of it? We do so only by contrast; by looking at our own experience of shame and flipping it over.

A woman does not feel the need to cover her body when she is alone in the shower. But if a strange man burst into the bathroom, she would. Why? John Paul II proposes that "shame" in this sense is a form of self-defense against being treated as an object for sexual use. In the case of this woman, she knows that she is never, ever meant to be treated as a "thing" for someone's kicks. Experience teaches her that men (because of the lust that resulted from original sin) tend to objectify women's bodies. Therefore, the woman covers her body not because it's "bad" or "shameful." She covers her body because it's good (very good!) and she fears that her goodness might be violated. She covers herself to protect her own dignity from the stranger's "lustful look"—a look that fails to respect her God-given dignity as a person.

Take this experience of fear in the presence of another person, flip it over, and we arrive at Adam and Eve's experience of nakedness *without* shame. Lust (self-seeking sexual desire) had not yet entered the human heart. Hence, our first parents experienced a total defenselessness in each other's presence because the other's look posed no threat whatsoever to their dignity. As John Paul II expresses, they "see and know each other . . . with all the peace of the interior gaze" (TOB 13:1). This interior gaze indicates not only the sight of a body, but a body that reveals a personal and spiritual mystery. They saw God's plan of love inscribed in their naked bodies, and *that is exactly what they desired*—to love as God loves in and through their bodies. And there is no fear in love. "Perfect love casts out fear" (1 John 4:18).

This is why nakedness without shame is the key for understanding God's plan for our lives—it reveals the original theology of our bodies and, through that, the truth of love. We need to let this point sink in: God gave us eros "in the beginning" to be the very power to love as he loves—in a free, sincere, and total gift of self. *This is how the couple described in Genesis experienced it.* Sexual desire was not felt as a compulsion or instinct for selfish gratification. The experience of lust comes only with the dawn of sin. Lust is a result of what we might call "flat-tire syndrome."

Since the first man and woman were "fully inflated" with God's love, they were entirely free to be a gift to one another. They were *"free with the very freedom of the gift,"* as John Paul II puts it (TOB 15:1). Only a person who is free from the compulsion of lust is capable of being a true "gift" to another. The freedom of the gift, then, is the freedom of the heart to *bless*, which is freedom from the compulsion to *grasp* and *possess*. It is this freedom that allowed the first couple to be naked without shame.

As a result of sin, our experience of erotic desire has become terribly distorted. In the midst of these distortions, we could think that there must be something wrong with sex and sexual desire itself (the "body-bad/sex-dirty" mentality stems from this). But the distortions we know so well are *not* at the core of sex. At the core of sex, we discover a sign of God's own goodness: "God saw everything that he had made, and behold, it was very good" (Genesis 1:31).

According to John Paul II, nakedness without shame demonstrates that the first couple participated in this same vision of God. They *knew* their goodness. They *knew* God's glorious plan of love. They *saw* it inscribed in their bodies, and they *experienced* it in their mutual desire (eros). We lost this glorious vision with the dawn of sin. But don't forget that "Jesus came to restore creation to the purity of its origins" (*CCC*, 2336). This will not be complete until heaven; yet through the gift of redemption, we can begin to reclaim what was lost even in this life.

The Spousal Meaning of the Body

Since lust so often holds sway in our fallen world, nakedness is often intertwined with all that is unholy. But in the beginning, John Paul II says it was nakedness that revealed God's holiness in the visible world. God's holiness is his eternal mystery of self-giving love—the eternal exchange of love among Father, Son, and Holy Spirit. Human holiness, in turn, is what enables "man to express himself deeply with his own body . . . precisely through the 'sincere gift' of self" (TOB 19:5).

Here John Paul II draws from another favorite passage from the Second Vatican Council: "Man can fully discover his true self only in a sincere giving of himself."[35] In other words, we can only discover who we are by loving as God loves. This, of course, is Christ's new commandment: "Love one another as I have loved you" (John 15:12). How did Christ love us? Recall his words at the Last Supper: "This is my body which is given for you" (Luke 22:19). Love is a spiritual reality, but as Christ demonstrates, love is expressed and realized *in the body*. In fact, God inscribed the call to divine love in our bodies—in our sexuality—right from the beginning.

In their nakedness, the first man and woman discovered what John Paul II calls "the spousal meaning of the body." Spousal love (we could also say marital, nuptial, or conjugal love) is the love of *total self-donation*. The spousal meaning of the body, therefore, is the body's *"power to express love: precisely that love in which the human person becomes a gift* and—through this gift—fulfills the very meaning of his being and existence" (TOB 15:1).

If you are looking for the meaning of life, according to John Paul II, it's impressed right in your body—in your sexuality! The purpose of life is to love as God loves and this is what your body as a man or woman calls you to. Think of it this way: A man's body doesn't make sense by itself. Nor does a woman's body. But seen in light of each other, sexual difference reveals the unmistakable plan of God that man and woman are meant to be a gift to one another.

Let's be more specific. A man's body is complete in all of its systems but one. A woman's body is complete in all of its systems but one. And those respective systems—the reproductive systems—only function in union with the other. We can see that man and woman are meant to be a gift to one another even at the cellular level. Every cell in a man's body has forty-six chromosomes . . . except for one. Every cell in a woman's body has forty-six chromosomes . . . except for one. The sperm cell and the ovum each have only twenty-three. Man and woman are meant to complete each other, and in the normal course of events, their reciprocal giving enables sperm and ovum to meet . . . and a third comes into existence. As John Paul II expresses it, "knowledge" leads to generation: "Adam *knew* his wife and she conceived" (Genesis 4:1).

Once again we see how the meaning of gender is rooted in our genitals, in the manner in which male and female depend on each other to bring about the next generation. Fatherhood and motherhood crown and completely reveal the mystery of sexuality. God's first directive in Genesis, "Be fruitful and multiply" (Genesis 1:28), is not merely an injunction to propagate. It's a call to love in God's image and thus fulfill the very meaning of our being and existence as engendered creatures.

The Fundamental Component of Existence

Marriage and procreation, of course, are not the only ways to love as God loves. They serve as the original model, but whenever we imitate Christ in giving up our bodies for others, we express the body's spousal meaning. Christ, in fact, will call some to sacrifice marriage "for the sake of the kingdom" (see Matthew 19:12). As we will see more clearly in chapter five, celibacy for the kingdom *is not a rejection of sexuality*. It's a call to embrace *the ultimate purpose and meaning of sexuality.* The one-flesh union is only a foreshadowing of something infinitely more grand and glorious—the eternal union of Christ and the Church (see Ephesians 5:31–32). Again, this will be clearer later on, but those who are given the charism of celibacy "skip" earthly marriage in order to devote themselves entirely to the heavenly marriage.

Whatever our particular vocation, we're all called to participate in God's love and share it with others. When we have the purity to see it, this is what the human body and human sexuality teach us. The spousal meaning of the body (that is, the call to love that God inscribed in our flesh) reveals what Vatican II describes as "the universal call to holiness." And yet how many people spurn their bodies and their sexuality in the name of a supposed holiness?

John Paul II observes that the spousal meaning of the body is an "indispensable theme" of our existence. In fact, it's "the fundamental component of human existence in the world" (TOB 15:5). Hence, whatever our state in life, the spousal meaning of the body is "indispensable for knowing who man is and who he ought to be" (TOB 18:4). Who we ought to be are men and women who love in the image of God. Tragically, sin has crippled us in our ability to love according to God's plan in the beginning. Even so, the spousal meaning of the body remains embedded in the fabric of our humanity as a call to restoration, a call to the redemption of the body that Christ has won for us. John Paul II observes that in the whole perspective of human history, we will not fail to confer a spousal meaning on our bodies. Even though the true meaning of the body undergoes many distortions, it will always remain at the deepest level of our humanity as a sign of the image of God. "Here we also find the road," he tells us, "that goes from the mystery of creation to the 'redemption of the body' (see Romans 8)" (TOB 15:5).

The more we enter into this redemption, the more we "discover and strengthen the bond that exists between the dignity of the human being (of the man or the woman) and the spousal meaning of his body" (TOB 86:8). And this is where John Paul II will take us in his next series of reflections.

FOR REFLECTION

1. How do you view your body? Be honest about areas where you've struggled. How does this fit with your understanding of holiness?

2. According to TOB, how is "true gender identity" expressed authentically?

3. How are you personally called to participate in God's love and express it to others through your body?

Thank you, Lord, that you created us to experience your love and share it with others. Thank you for creating us with bodies that are designed to do just that.

THREE

The Redemption of the Body

What if we didn't see passion and desire as such as the problem, but rather sought to redirect it? . . . The erotic—even misdirected eros—is a sign of the kinds of animals we are: creatures who desire God.

—James K. A. Smith

We began the last chapter with a reflection on the wise men and the courage it took to recognize the star as a sign of something divine and embark on a journey to find God in the flesh. This is the same journey the priest was inviting the young lovers on when he asked them what their passion had to do with the stars.

Wise men (and women) are precisely those who know how to recognize small "b" beauty as a sign of capital "B" Beauty. They are able to recognize in all the wonders of creation so many signs of God himself. In fact, the Book of Wisdom defines a fool as one "who from the good things seen did not succeed in knowing him who is, and from studying [God's] works did not succeed in knowing the artisan" (Wisdom 13:1, NAB).

St. Paul picks up on this theme in his letter to the Romans. Speaking of those who did not recognize God's "invisible nature" in and through the visible things he had created, he says, "Claiming to be wise, they became fools." They "exchanged the glory of the immortal God for images resembling mortal man" (Romans 1:22–23). Interestingly, St. Paul says that this exchange of God's glory for human images is the root of sexual lust: "Therefore God gave them up in the lusts of their hearts to impurity, to the dishonoring of their bodies among themselves, because they exchanged the truth of God for a lie and worshiped and served the creature rather than the Creator" (Romans 1:24–25).

Redirecting Eros Toward the Infinite

We worship whatever we think will satisfy our deepest desires. Eros yearns for the infinite, crying out to be "filled with all the fullness of God" (Ephesians 3:19). In the divine plan, sexual love is meant to point us to the infinite and open us up to it. But when we fail to see our sexuality as a sign that leads beyond itself to the mystery of God, eros gets "stuck" on the body itself, and we come to expect small "b" beauty to do what only capital "B" Beauty is capable of: fulfilling our deepest longings. This, according to the Bible, is the very essence of idolatry, and the very essence of sexual lust. Still, behind every false god is the desire for the true God gone awry. And this means that even misdirected eros tells us the kind of beings we are—creatures who long for infinite Beauty but who often get stuck on its finite reflection.

The gospel does not call us to retreat from erotic longing, but to press into it *as deeply as possible* so as to rediscover it as a longing for the infinite, as a longing for God. As Pope Benedict XVI expressed it, erotic longing at its depths "leads to being drawn out and finding oneself before the mystery that encompasses the whole of existence." It becomes a pilgrimage "towards authentic self-discovery and indeed the discovery of God."[36]

It's the distortion of sin that causes us to experience eros as a base impulse dragging us down toward what is false, faulty, and foul. Christ came to redeem eros so that we could rediscover it as "the upward impulse of the human spirit toward what is true, good, and beautiful" (TOB 48:1). In fact, salvation begins right here—with the redemption of eros. As papal preacher Father Raniero Cantalamessa stated, Christ has "come to 'save' the world, beginning from eros, which is the dominant force."[37]

Think about it: Where did Jesus perform his first miracle? Recall that a married couple ran out of wine at their own wedding banquet. Recall also that, throughout the Bible, wine is a symbol of divine love (agape). Since the dawn of sin, eros has been cut off from agape. Or, to go with the symbolism of Cana, eros has "run out of wine." Christ's first miracle is to restore the wine to eros in superabundance. And he wants us to drink up! "Let anyone who is thirsty come to me and drink!" (John 7:37).

Do you know what the goal of the Christian life is from this perspective? It's to get utterly plastered on God's wine. Isn't that what the crowd accused the apostles of on Pentecost when the fire of God's love descended upon them? "You guys are drunk!" (see Acts 2:13–15). That's where John Paul II invites us in this section of his reflections: to a holy intoxication on God's wine so that our entire humanity—body and soul, sexuality and spirituality—becomes enflamed with divine love.

The Experience of Lust

John Paul II reflects at great length on what he calls the "historical" experience of the body and sexuality. History, in this sense of the term, begins with original sin and marks a dramatic departure from "the beginning." Christ speaks directly to this experience when he appeals to the human heart in the Sermon on the Mount: "You have heard that it was said, 'You shall not commit adultery.' But I say to you that everyone who looks at a woman lustfully has already committed adultery with her in his heart" (Matthew 5:27–28). This is the second of the three key words John Paul II reflects on in his TOB.

For the sake of example, Christ speaks directly of male lust, but the principle applies equally to women. Most would agree that male lust is often geared toward physical gratification at the expense of a woman, while female lust is often geared toward a kind of emotional gratification at the expense of a man. Of course, women have physical cravings just as men have emotional ones, but the saying that "men will use love in order to get sex and women will use sex in order to feel loved" seems to capture something about the way men and women are wired.

It's also true that some men and women experience lust for their own sex. While homosexuality is a complex and sensitive matter that deserves further treatment than we can offer here, we can at least provide an initial outline of how the TOB illuminates this particular issue. First, we can and must affirm all that is true, good, and beautiful about eros in the human heart—including the rightful attraction we should all have toward the goodness of our own sex. However, we must also recognize that eros has been disoriented in each of us by original sin. This means that the way to attain the love we long for isn't simply by submitting to our erotic desires as we now experience them. That's a recipe not for love, but for using others for our selfish pleasures. The fact of the matter is that each and every one of us is in need of sexual "re-orientation" according to God's original plan for making us male and female.

The beginning, before sin, is the norm for a proper understanding of sexuality. Hence, Christ's proclamation—"from the beginning it was not so" (Matthew 19:8)—is decisive not just for divorce, but for every other way the human heart has veered from God's original plan. The homosexual inclination is just one in a very long list of inclinations that stem from our fallen condition. While it's true that these inclinations are inherited with our fallen humanity and not chosen, it's equally true that we can chose whether to foster or to fight these inclinations. We're *all* called to the spiritual battle involved in following Christ; we're *all* called to the purification and healing of our desires. This entails discipline and self-denial, but it's a discipline that's authentically liberating and constructive, not repressive and destructive.

The *healing and restoration of God's original plan for eros*—that's what Christ's words about lust in the Sermon on the Mount are all about. And they apply equally to everyone—however our fallen inclinations might manifest themselves. Through Christ's appeal to our hearts we *"must rediscover the lost fullness of [our] humanity and want to regain it"* (TOB 43:7). And there is real power flowing from Christ's words to enable us to do so. It isn't easy. And it doesn't happen overnight. Like Paul we may carry a particular "thorn" of weakness in our flesh throughout our earthly journey (see 2 Corinthians 12:7). Even so, God's grace is sufficient for us to remain faithful to his original "very good" design for our sexuality.

And so we can see again that the Theology of the Body is for everybody, regardless of a person's particular struggles. In short, by taking proper account of the beginning, the fall, and the redemption, the TOB saves us from the strong temptation of normalizing our brokenness, as if God made us that way. It's okay that we're broken. Everyone is. God loves us right there and comes to meet us right there. But it's not okay to call our brokenness health. So long as we do, we remain closed to God's remedy, like a sick man who sees no need for a doctor because he refuses to admit that he's ill.

Lord, as we continue our study of your saving words, open our hearts to your healing power!

Looking with Lust

When Christ speaks of looking with lust, he's not saying that a mere glance or momentary thought makes us guilty of adultery. As fallen human beings, we will always be able to sense the pull of lust in our hearts and in our bodies. This doesn't mean that we have sinned. It's what we do when we experience the pull of lust that matters. Do we seek God's help in resisting it or do we indulge it? When we indulge it—that is, when we actively choose "in our hearts" to treat another person as merely an object for our own gratification—we seriously violate that person's dignity and our own. We're meant to be loved for our own sakes, and never to be used as an object for someone else's sake. Don't we know this in our own hearts? The opposite of love in this case is not hatred; rather, the opposite of love is to *use* someone as a means to our own selfish ends.

Furthermore, it's significant that Christ refers to looking lustfully at "a woman." He doesn't restrict his words to someone other than a spouse. As John Paul II observes, a man commits "adultery in the heart" not only by looking lustfully at a woman he is not married to, "but *precisely* because he looks in this way at a woman. Even if he were to look in this way at . . . his wife, he would commit the same adultery 'in the heart'" (TOB 43:2). In other words, marriage does *not* justify lust. It doesn't make *using* your spouse okay.

Few Christian men understand this crucial point. The books and programs that have flooded the Christian market to help us in our "pornified" culture rarely get this either. The main thrust of these programs is to help husbands direct their sexual desires toward their wives—a good first step, of course. But rarely, if ever, do these programs invite men to examine *what kind of desires* they're directing toward their wives. I recall reviewing one such program that, in attempting to relieve husbands of the guilt they sometimes feel for the sexual demands they make on their wives, suggested that men should feel no more pang of conscience in this regard than they do in wanting to eat a cheeseburger. While a certain comparison can be made between hunger and sexual desire, do you notice that this analogy reduces the wife to a piece of meat? If a man approaches his wife as an object of consumption, it's not love at work, but lust.

I don't want to harp on us men too much here. Women's drives have also become deeply disordered by original sin, and this wreaks havoc in the lives of men. Still, John Paul II maintains that men have a "special responsibility" to restore the balance of love in the male-female relationship. It's "as if it depended more on him whether the balance is kept or violated or even—if it has already been violated—reestablished" (TOB 33:2). A critical part of this reestablishment is for spouses to reexamine the motives with which they approach one another for sex.

No doubt, in response to this challenge, some men will want to appeal to various Scripture verses that seem to justify a different approach. But if we want to be honest about St. Paul's teaching on submission (see Ephesians 5:22–23) and the marital duty (1 Corinthians 7:3–5), then we must recognize that our marital duty—as Paul states quite clearly—is to love our wives "as Christ loved the Church" (Ephesians 5:25). Submitting ourselves to that means there is no justification for treating our wives as objects. The sexual embrace is meant to image and express divine love. This is what Paul calls us to in his letters, and this is what Christ calls us to in his words about lust in the Sermon on the Mount. These words show us "how deep down it is necessary to go, how the innermost recesses of the human heart must be thoroughly revealed, so that this heart might become a place in which the law [of love] is 'fulfilled'" (TOB 43:5).

Not even the holiest of spouses live the "law of love" perfectly in this regard, but it's critical that we commit ourselves to the journey of allowing God's mercy and grace to transform our hearts. Otherwise, "making love" amounts to little more than "making lust," and this wounds us terribly.

Words of Salvation, Not Condemnation

John Paul II acknowledges that Christ's words about lust are severe. But, he asks, are we to fear his words, or rather have confidence in their power to save us (see TOB 43:7)? Most people see in the severity of Christ's words only a condemnation. Do we forget that he came not to condemn but to save (see John 3:17)?

Christ is calling us to "enter our full image" (see TOB 25:2). The heritage of original sin has obscured the image of God in us. But John Paul II insists that the heritage of our hearts is *deeper* than the sinfulness we've inherited, and if we're honest with ourselves, we still desire what's deeper. If the human heart is a deep well, it's true that there are layers and layers of sludge. But if we press through the mud and the mire, at the bottom of the well we find a spring that, when activated, can fill the well to overflowing with pure, living water. This spring is the deeper heritage of our hearts. John Paul II proclaims that the words of Christ reactivate that deeper heritage, giving it *real power* in our lives (see TOB 46:6).

This means that we needn't walk through life merely coping with our lusts and disorders. Christ didn't die on a cross and rise from the dead to give us more coping mechanisms for our sins. We already had plenty of those without a savior. Christ died on a cross and rose from the dead to save us from sin so that we, too, could live a new life (see Romans 6:4). Again, we need to stress that this "new life" will only come to fulfillment in the resurrection at the end of time; "but it is also true that, in a certain way, we have already risen with Christ" (*CCC*, 1002). Here and now we can begin to experience the redemption of our sexual desires, the transformation of our hearts. It's a difficult and even arduous journey full of peaks and valleys, victories and setbacks. But it's a journey that can be undertaken. God's grace is enough for us!

Questioning God's Gift

If we are to experience the redemption of our sexuality, we must first examine how and why we fell from God's original plan for it. So, once again, John Paul II takes us back to Genesis, this time to examine the nature of the original sin and the entrance of the fig leaves.

He describes original sin as "the questioning of the gift." Allow me to explain. The deepest yearning of the human heart is to be like God by sharing in his life and love. Right from the beginning, God had granted man and woman a sharing in his own life and love as a totally free gift. Using the spousal image, God *initiated* the gift of himself as Bridegroom, and man (male and female) opened to *receive* the gift as Bride. In turn, man and woman were able to reimage this same exchange of love through their own marital self-giving and unity.

In order to retain this divine likeness and remain in his love, God asked only that they not eat from "the tree of the knowledge of good and evil." If they did eat of it, they would cut themselves off from the source of life and love. In other words, they would die (see Genesis 2:16–17).

Sounds simple enough. So where did it all go wrong? "Behind the disobedient choice of our first parents lurks a seductive voice, opposed to God, which makes them fall into death out of envy. Scripture and the Church's Tradition see in this being a fallen angel, called 'Satan' or the 'devil'" (*CCC*, 391). Satan's an incredibly knowledgeable being. He knows that God created the union of the sexes as a sharing in divine life, and his goal is to keep us from this. So he aims his attack at *"the very heart of that unity that had, from the 'beginning,' been formed by man and woman*, created and called to become 'one flesh'" (TOB 20:1).

Having approached the woman—the one who represents us all as "bride" in our *receptivity* to God's gift—the serpent insists, "You will not die [if you eat from the forbidden tree]. For God knows that when you eat of it your eyes will be opened, and you will be like God, knowing good and evil" (Genesis 3:4–5). We might read the serpent's temptation like this: "God doesn't love you. He's not looking out for you. He's a tyrant, a slave driver who wants to keep you from what you really want. That's why he told you not to eat from that tree. If you want life and happiness, if you want to be 'like God,' then you have to reach out and *take* it for yourself because God sure won't give it to you."

Herein lies the *questioning*—and, ultimately, the denial—of God's gift. In the moment they reject their *receptivity* before God and *grasp* at their own "happiness," they turn their backs on God's love, on God's gift. In a way, they cast God's love out of their hearts. "Then the eyes of both were opened, and they knew that they were naked; and they sewed fig leaves together and made themselves aprons" (Genesis 3:7).

The tendency to "grasp" seems built in to our fallen nature. We can observe it even in little children. For example, when my son asks for a cookie for dessert, before I can even get the cookie out of the box to present it to him as a gift, what does he do? He *grasps* at it. Taking advantage of this teachable moment, I might say to my son, "Hold on, you're denying the gift. Your papa loves you. I want to *give* this cookie to you as a gift. If you believed in the gift, all you would need to do is hold your hands out in confidence and *receive* the cookie as a gift." This is the problem with us all. We do not trust enough in our Father's love, so we grasp at the "cookie."

The Second Discovery of Sex

God said that if Adam and Eve ate from the tree, they would die. They didn't keel over dead, but they did die spiritually. In the act of creation, God had *in*spired their bodies, breathing in his own life and love (see Genesis 2:7). Now their bodies *ex*pired, that is, they breathed out God's Spirit. This is the precise moment they "ran out of wine," the precise moment eros "ran out" of agape (divine love).

At this point, a basic principle kicked in: *You can't give what you don't have.* The purpose of the sexual relationship is to share divine love, but they no longer had it to share. What was left? Lust. Having denied the gift in their relationship with God, they no longer experienced sexual desire as the power to be a gift to one another. Instead, they desired to *grasp* and *possess* one another for their own gratification. As John Paul II says, with the dawn of lust, the *"relationship of the gift changes into a relationship of appropriation"* (TOB 32:6). To "appropriate" in this sense means "to take hold of" with the desire to *use*.

John Paul II calls this "the second discovery of sex," and it differs radically from the first (see TOB 29:4). In the first discovery of sex, Adam and Eve experienced total peace and harmony. Now they immediately felt threatened. Nakedness originally revealed their Godlike dignity. Now they instinctively hid their nakedness from the other's look.

Shame, therefore, has a double meaning. It indicates that we have lost sight of the spousal meaning of our bodies (God's plan of love stamped in our sexuality), but it also indicates an inherent need to *protect* the spousal meaning of the body from the degradation of lust. As John Paul II poetically expresses it, lust "tramples on the ruins" of the spousal meaning of the body and aims directly to satisfy only the "sexual need" of the body (see TOB 40:4). It seeks "the sensation of sexuality" apart from a true gift of self and a true communion of persons. Lust, in fact, shatters their communion.

Lust is often thought of as some benefit to the sexual relationship or perceived as an *increase* or *intensification* of sexual desire. In reality, lust is a *reduction* of the original fullness God intended for erotic desire. We don't get "more" when we lust, but much less. Eros, Pope Benedict tells us, is meant "to provide not just fleeting pleasure, but a certain foretaste of the pinnacle of our existence, of that beatitude [bliss and happiness] for which our whole being yearns."[38]

If eros is meant to lead us to an infinite banquet of love and satisfaction, lust reduces eros to a craving for "fast food"— immediate gratification that may taste good going down, but ultimately leaves us feeling poisoned and used. Indulgence of lust can't possibly reach us where we yearn to be reached, where the ache continues to gnaw at us, where the cry of the heart remains as haunting as ever.

Why would we ever choose the fast food over the divine banquet? Because we've denied the gift. We don't really believe God wants to satisfy our desires. That's the original sin: We "exchanged the truth about God for a lie" (Romans 1:25) and came to believe that God was holding out on us.

"You see, man strives for eternal joy; he would like pleasure in the extreme," observes Benedict XVI. But when we believe God is holding out on us, we ourselves "must now create something that is fictitious, a false eternity."[39] Our desire for "eternal joy," for "pleasure in the extreme" isn't the problem; God created us that way. Our problem, once again, is that we've come to believe the satisfaction of our hunger (eros) is totally up to us: that God is not going to come through for us. Fast food becomes our false eternity, our momentary, but fleeting satisfaction. Shame, in turn, is the result of a deep, interior knowing that something is dreadfully amiss.

"I was afraid, because I was naked; so I hid myself" (Genesis 3:10). From this moment on, shame will cause "a fundamental disquiet in the whole of human existence" (TOB 28:3). Shame, in fact, touches man and woman at their "deepest level and seems to shake the very foundations of their existence" (TOB 27:1). In a way, by covering their bodies with fig leaves (precisely those parts of their bodies that distinguish them and call them to unite), man and woman blame their bodies for lust. But such an approach is quite literally a "cover-up"—almost an excuse not to face the deep disorder of their hearts.

As Jesus stresses in the Sermon on the Mount, lust is first and foremost a problem of the heart, not the body. Until we address the disordered desires of our hearts, we will never be able to live as the men and women God created us to be. As we observed previously, lust tends to affect the male and female personality differently, but the hearts of both men and women have become a battlefield between love and lust (see TOB 32:3).

Christian Ethos: Morality from the Heart

Conforming our behavior to an external norm is not enough. We all know it is possible to follow "the rules" without ever attaining holiness (that is, without a heart "in-spired" by God's love). This kind of rigid and lifeless conformity to rules is called "legalism" or "moralism." In the Sermon on the Mount, Christ calls us to something *very* different. He calls us to a living morality that flows from the heart.

Jesus sets the stage for this new morality by saying, "Unless your righteousness exceeds that of the scribes and the Pharisees, you will never enter the kingdom of heaven" (Matthew 5:20). What could these words have sounded like to the Jews who heard them? The Scribes and the Pharisees were considered the most righteous of all. But for many of them, at least the ones Jesus singled out, it was all external. They conformed to the ethic, but their ethos remained skewed.

An *ethic* is an external norm or rule—"do this," "don't do that." *Ethos* refers to a person's inner world of values, what attracts and repulses him deep in the heart. In the Sermon on the Mount, Christ is not only confirming God's ethical code, he is also proclaiming the true *ethos* of God's commandments—what they call us to *internally*. In effect, Christ says, "You've heard the ethic not to commit adultery, but the problem is you *desire* to commit adultery. Your *ethos* is flawed because you're filled with lust."

It seems almost cruel. Knowing we are filled with lust, Jesus says, "Don't lust." Great! So what are we supposed to do? Christ holds out a standard he knows we cannot meet. It seems hopeless—*unless* . . . unless it were possible to experience some kind of redemption or transformation of our desires. This is precisely where the Gospel becomes *good news*. As John Paul II repeatedly stresses, the new ethos that Christ proclaims in the Sermon on the Mount is not only given to us as a task. It is also given as a gift. We are not left to our own flaws, weaknesses, and sinfulness. In the "Sermon on the Mount . . . the Spirit of the Lord gives new form to our desires, those inner movements that animate our lives" (*CCC*, 2764).

As John Paul II puts it, "Christian ethos is characterized by a transformation of the human person's conscience and attitudes . . . such as to express and realize the value of the body and sex according to the Creator's original plan" (TOB 45:3). What good news! What hope! What joy! We are not *bound* by lust. The new dimension of *ethos* is always connected with the heart's liberation from lust (see TOB 43:6). And through this liberation a "person can certainly channel his passions in a beautiful and healthy way, increasingly pointing them towards altruism and an integrated self-fulfillment," says Pope Francis. "This does not mean renouncing moments of intense enjoyment, but rather integrating them with [the truth of love]."[40] In this way we experience "a living morality," John Paul II says, in which we realize the very meaning of our humanity (see TOB 24:3).

Freedom from the Law

Most people look at Christian morality—especially sexual morality—as an oppressive list of rules to follow. How far this (mis)understanding is from the living morality proclaimed by Christ! "Christian morality is not a form of stoicism," insists Pope Francis, "or a catalogue of sins and faults. Before all else, the Gospel invites us to respond to the God of love who saves us."[41] What does he save us from? Among other things, Christ came to save us from the oppression of the law, of the rules. The Gospel doesn't give us more rules to follow. The Gospel is meant to *change our hearts* so that we no longer need the rules (see *CCC*, 1968). To the degree that we experience this change of heart, we experience "freedom from the law" (see Romans 7; Galatians 5)—not freedom to break the law, but freedom to *fulfill* it.

Here's an example of what freedom from the law looks like: Do you have any desire to murder your best friend? This may seem like an odd question, but it actually demonstrates the point. Assuming you do not, then you do not need the commandment "Thou shalt not murder thy best friend," because you have no desire to break it. To this extent you are free from the law. In other words, you do not experience this law ("Thou shalt not murder thy best friend") as an imposition because your heart already conforms to it.

Before sin, the human heart conformed totally to God's will. For example, the first married couple did not need a law forbidding adultery. They had no desire to commit adultery (and not only because there was no one else around). Only with original sin do we experience a rupture between our desires and God's will for us. Here is where the law serves its essential purpose. It is given to convict us of sin (see Romans 7:7). However, when Christ says "You have heard the commandment . . . but I tell you . . ." he indicates that we need something more than mere precepts can offer.

The Old Testament law is good and just, but it "does not of itself give the strength, the grace of the Spirit, to fulfill it" (CCC, 1963). In other words, the law convicts us of having "run out of wine," but it does not restore it. "The Law of the Gospel," however, "proceeds to reform the heart, the root of human acts, where man chooses between the pure and the impure" (CCC, 1968). To the degree that we allow Christ to restore the wine in our lives we no longer need the law because we no longer desire to break it; we are "free from the law."

Here's a question we can ask ourselves to determine where our hearts still need to be liberated: What laws do we still need? What teachings of the Church feel like a burden or imposition? Perhaps the problem is not with the law or with the Church, but with our own hardness of heart. If this is where we find ourselves, the solution is not to toss off the law. The solution is to surrender our disordered desires to Christ and let him transform them.

Trying to follow all the rules without opening our hearts to the new wine is futile. Those who do either will become self-righteous hypocrites or will abandon God's law for a rationalized, watered-down version of the Gospel. Either way, it's a "gospel" without the good news; it's Christianity without Christ. Both the self-righteous and the lawless have yet to pass over from the bondage of the ethical code to the freedom of the new ethos—the freedom of redemption.

Such freedom liberates us not from the *external* constraint that calls us to good, but from the *internal* constraint that hinders our choice of the good. When we *desire* what is true, good, and beautiful, then we are free indeed—free to love, free to bless, free from the compulsion to *grasp* and *possess*. Those who toss off the law in order to indulge their lusts may imagine themselves free, but like an alcoholic who cannot say "no" to the bottle, a person who cannot say "no" to lust is *enslaved*. "For freedom Christ has set us free; stand fast therefore, and do not submit again to a yoke of slavery" (Galatians 5:1).

The Grace of Creation Becomes the Grace of Redemption

As John Paul II says, living in this freedom "is a still uncertain and fragile journey as long as we are on earth, but it is one made possible by grace, which enables us to possess the full freedom of the children of God (see Romans 8:21)."[42] We are not justified by the law. We are "justified by . . . grace as a gift, through the redemption which is in Christ" (Romans 3:24).

What is grace? John Paul II describes it as God's mysterious gift to the human heart that enables men and women to live in the reciprocal and sincere gift of self (see TOB 16:3). In the beginning, man and woman were infused with grace; they were drunk on God's wine. When they doubted God's love and denied the gift, they fell from grace and "ran out of wine." If this is the source of the problem, what is the first step toward a solution? Faith. If original sin is our denial of God's gift, "*faith*, in its deepest essence, is *the openness* of the human heart to the gift: *to God's self-communication in the Holy Spirit.*"[43]

John Paul II observes that when Christ calls us to overcome lust in the Sermon on the Mount, his words bear witness that the original grace of creation has become for each of us the grace of redemption (see TOB 46:5). The Son of God took on flesh and died on a cross so that our sinfulness might be put to death. He rose from the dead to re-create us. He ascended into heaven with his glorified body to "in-spire" our bodies once again with God's life and love. Through this gift of our redemption, Christ breathes back into our flesh that same Spirit (grace) that "ex-spired" from our bodies when we denied the gift (see John 20:22). Through this gift of our redemption, he pours his wine of agape back into our eros.

Repent and Believe in the Good News

Many people, especially those raised with a legalistic form of religiosity like myself, have grown up with the impression that love is something earned by good behavior: I'm lovable if I'm "good" and I'm unlovable if I'm not. Within this terribly faulty paradigm, it can be very difficult to accept the merciful love of God. Jesus' whole life bears witness to the truth that God loves unconditionally; he is unequivocally *for* us, not against us. His whole life demonstrates that the banquet of love we hunger for really exists. We don't have to earn it—it's a completely free, utterly gratuitous gift! And everyone without exception is invited.

In essence, Christ's life proclaims: "You don't believe God loves you? Let me stretch out my arms and show you how much God loves you. You don't believe that God is 'gift'? This is my body given for you (see Luke 22:19). You think God wants to keep you from life? I will offer myself so that my life's blood can give you life to the full (see John 10:10). You thought God was a tyrant, a slave driver? I will take the form of a slave (see Philippians 2:7); I will let you lord it over me to demonstrate that God has no desire to lord it over you (see Matthew 20:28). You thought God would whip your back if you gave him the chance? I will let you whip my back to demonstrate that God has no desire to whip yours. I have not come to condemn you but to save you (see John 3:17). I have not come to enslave you but to set you free (see Galatians 5:1). Stop persisting in your unbelief. Repent and believe in the good news" (see Mark 1:15).

As we open ourselves to this gift, the grace of redemption begins to revivify our humanity, to enliven our hearts with God's own goodness. To the degree that we allow this grace to inform and *transform* us, the Holy Spirit impregnates our sexual desires "with everything that is noble and beautiful," with "the supreme value which is love" (TOB 46:5).

Where is the grace of redemption poured out? Primarily in the sacramental life of the Church. Sacraments are not merely religious rituals. They infuse holiness into the terrain of our humanity: they penetrate our soul and body, our femininity and masculinity, with the power of holiness (see TOB 117b:2). In other words, sacraments make Christ's death and resurrection a *living reality* in our own lives. Unfortunately, many Christians fail to tap into the power of the sacraments. Through baptism alone, it's as if we've been given a trillion dollars in our bank accounts, but few of us seem to withdraw more than about seventy-five cents. In the sacraments, God's love is "poured into our hearts through the Holy Spirit" (Romans 5:5). We need to *bank* on this gift.

Life in the Spirit and the Redemption of the Body

In the apostle Paul's terminology, living the life of grace is synonymous with living "according to the Spirit." He contrasts this with "living according to the flesh." Walk "by the Spirit, and do not gratify the desires of the flesh. For the desires of the flesh are against the Spirit, and the desires of the Spirit are against the flesh" (Galatians 5:16–17).

This does *not* mean, as many have tragically concluded, that St. Paul condemns the body or thinks of it as an inherent obstacle to living a "spiritual" life. As we have already learned in our study of John Paul II's teaching, the body is the specific vehicle of the spiritual life. In this context, "the flesh" refers to the whole person (body and soul) cut off from God's inspiration, cut off from God's indwelling Spirit. It refers to a person dominated by lust and the other vices. In turn, the person who lives "according to the Spirit" does *not* reject his body, but opens his whole body-soul personality to divine inspiration.

With great hope, John Paul II proclaims that as much as lust enslaves us by disordering our passions, so much does this "life according to the Spirit" free us to be a gift to others. As much as lust blinds us to the truth of God's plan for the body, so much does life according to the Spirit open our eyes to the body's spousal meaning (see TOB 101:5). So, to the degree that we open ourselves to life in the Spirit, we also experience "the redemption of our bodies" (Romans 8:23).

John Paul II insists that the redemption of the body is not only a heavenly reality. We await its fulfillment then, but it is already at work in us now. This means that as we allow our lusts to be "crucified with Christ" (see Galatians 5:24), "sexuality can be experienced as a sharing in the full life of the resurrection."[44] And that "full life" allows us progressively to rediscover in what is erotic that original spousal meaning of the body and live it. John Paul II tells us that this liberation from lust and the freedom it affords is, in fact, the condition for living all of life together in the truth (see TOB 43:6).

Purity Is Not Prudishness

To the degree that we live the redemption of our bodies, we understand that sexual purity is not a matter of annihilating or repressing sexual attraction and desire. Rather, mature purity "consists in quickness to affirm the value of the person in every situation, and in raising [sexual reactions] to the personal level."[45] In the Sermon on the Mount, Christ is not simply saying, "Don't look." John Paul II explains that Jesus' words are "an invitation to a pure way of looking at others, capable of respecting the spousal meaning of the body."[46]

Obviously, if a person needs to turn away in order to avoid lusting, then, by all means, "don't look." For the person who is bound by lust, the Old Testament admonition, "Turn away your eyes from a shapely woman" (Sirach 9:8), retains all its wisdom. We classically call this "avoiding the occasion of sin" by "gaining custody of the eyes." This is a necessary first step, but John Paul II would describe such an approach as a "negative" purity. As we grow in virtue we come to experience "positive" or "mature" purity. In mature purity we enjoy the fruits of the victory won over lust. We enjoy the "efficacy of the gift of the Holy Spirit," who restores to our experience of the body "all *its simplicity, its lucid clarity*, and also *its interior joy*" (TOB 58:7).

Practically everyone begins the journey toward mature purity on the negative side. Unfortunately, many people stagnate at this stage, thinking it's all they can expect. Keep going! Needless to say, I am far from being a perfect man; living the TOB is a daily challenge, and I've fallen in more ways than I'd like to admit. At the same time, in the midst of the struggle, I can attest to the fact that as we appropriate the gift of redemption in our lives, lust loses sway in our hearts. We come not only to understand, but to *see* and *experience* the body as a "theology," a sign of God's own mystery. "Blessed are the pure in heart, for they shall see God" (Matthew 5:8). If we understand what John Paul II is holding out to us here, we can add: "Blessed are the pure in heart, for they shall see God's mystery revealed through the human body."

Purity, therefore, is not prudishness. It does *not* reject the body. "Purity is the glory of the human body before God. It is the glory of God in the human body, through which masculinity and femininity are manifested" (TOB 57:3). Purity in its fullness will only be restored in heaven. Yet, as the *Catechism* teaches, "Even now [purity of heart] enables us to see *according to* God . . . it lets us perceive the human body—ours and our neighbor's—as a temple of the Holy Spirit, a manifestation of divine beauty" (*CCC*, 2519).

The Christian who denies that this kind of purity is possible will either justify his (or her) lusts or remain locked in the rule-obsessed religiosity of the Pharisees. The Pharisees were "constantly stumbling into passersby," writes Father Alexander Men. "They were afraid to lift their eyes lest they should accidentally look upon a woman. They were called in jest *Khitsay*, 'don't-hit-your-head.' It is natural that Christ's freedom should have irritated and frightened such people; they saw in it temptation and threat to their good morals."[47]

And this, sadly, is how many people view the freedom to which John Paul II is calling us in his TOB. Many "religious" people, for example, found themselves scandalized by his decision to have several of the loincloths removed from the figures in the Sistine Chapel (loincloths that previous popes had ordered to be painted over Michelangelo's original nudes). And he did this in the name of Christian purity! During the homily dedicating the restored frescos, John Paul II proclaimed the Sistine Chapel *"the sanctuary of the theology of the human body."* He added, "It seems that Michelangelo, in his own way, allowed himself to be guided by the evocative words of the Book of Genesis which . . . reveals: 'The man and his wife were both naked, yet felt no shame' (Genesis 2:25)."[48]

What, then, is the difference between pornography and a proper artistic portrayal of nakedness? John Paul II says the difference lies in the intention of the artist. Pornographic portrayals of the body raise objection "not because of their object, because in itself the human body always has its own inalienable dignity— but because of the quality or way of its artistic reproduction" (TOB 63:5). The pornographer seeks only to arouse lust in the viewer, while the true artist (such as Michelangelo) helps us see "the whole personal mystery of man." Proper portrayals of the naked body can teach us "the spousal meaning of the body which corresponds to, and provides the measure for 'purity of heart'" (TOB 63:5). Those who experience mature purity understand the naked body for what it is—the revelation of God's plan of love. And with God they can joyfully and freely exclaim, "Behold, it is very good!" (see Genesis 1:31).

The Interpretation of Suspicion

Doubters respond, "Impossible! The naked body will always arouse lust." For the person dominated by lust, this is true. But "of which man are we speaking?" asks John Paul II. "Of man *dominated by lust* or of man *redeemed by Christ*? This is what is at stake: the *reality* of Christ's redemption. *Christ has redeemed us!* This means he has given us the possibility of realizing the *entire truth* of our being; he has set our freedom free from the *domination* of lust."[49]

As he wrote in *Love and Responsibility*, we cannot simply equate nakedness with immodesty and lust. Immodesty is certainly present "when nakedness plays a negative role with regard to the value of the person, when its aim is to arouse [lust]." But, he added, "this is not inevitable."[50] If we think a lustful look is the only way a person *can* look at the human body, then we subscribe to what John Paul II calls "the interpretation of suspicion." Those who live by suspicion remain so locked in their own lusts that they project the same bondage on everyone else. They cannot imagine any way to think about the human body and the sexual relationship other than through the prism of lust.

When, because of lust, we hold the human heart in "a state of continual and irreversible suspicion" (TOB 46:4), we condemn ourselves to a hopeless, loveless existence. We condemn ourselves to a pharisaical religiosity of external conformity to the rules (*ethics*) without a change of heart (*ethos*). When this is the overriding religious milieu, it's only a matter of time before the pendulum swings to the other extreme (think sexual revolution). As John Paul II wrote, in the history of man's evaluation of his own body and sexuality, "he passes from the pole of pessimism to the pole of optimism, from puritanical strictness to present-day permissiveness" (TOB 44:4).

Both extremes are bound by the same suspicion—the idea that lust is the only paradigm for sexuality. One represses it while the other revels in it. One typically denies religion altogether while the other holds "the form of religion" but denies "the power of it" (2 Timothy 3:5).

If Christians themselves don't believe in the power of redemption to transform eros, what do we have to offer a sexually indulgent world other than rules and repression? If the contest is between the starvation diet and the fast food, the fast food wins hands down. But if redemption can truly redirect our desires toward a divine banquet that infinitely satisfies our hunger, the banquet wins hands down.

As John Paul II boldly proclaims: "Redemption is a truth, a reality, in the name of which man must feel called, and 'called with effectiveness'" (TOB 46:4). The death and resurrection of Christ is truly *effective*: It can change our lives, our attitudes, our hearts, and—yes—the way we experience our sexual desires. "*Do not empty the cross of its power!*" (see 1 Corinthians 1:17), John Paul II exclaims. This "is the cry of the new evangelization."[51]

Much is at stake. "The meaning of life is the antithesis of the [interpretation] 'of suspicion.'" This interpretation "is very different, *it is radically different* from the one we discover *in Christ's words* in the Sermon on the Mount. These words bring to light . . . another vision of man's possibilities" (TOB 46:6). Unless we tap into this other vision of man's possibilities, we will find it impossible to love as Christ loves; we will remain cut off from the meaning of life.

Growing in Mature Purity

So how do we tap into this other vision of man's possibilities? How do we progress from negative purity to positive? I will begin with a quote from John Paul II and then add some personal reflections.

To grow in purity, John Paul II says that we must devote ourselves to "a progressive education in self-control of the will, of sentiments, of emotions, which must be developed from the simplest gestures, in which it is relatively easy to put the inner decision into practice" (TOB 128:1). For example, what are your eating habits? If you cannot say no to a potato chip, how are you going to say no to indulging in lust? Fasting is a wonderful way to grow in mastery of our passions. If this is not already part of your life, start with a simple sacrifice that's relatively easy to put into practice. As you continue exercising this "muscle," you will find your strength increasing. What was once impossible gradually becomes possible.

The muscle analogy, however, is only half right. Growing in purity certainly demands human effort, but we are also aided by supernatural grace. Here it's crucial to distinguish between indulgence, repression, and redemption. When lust flares up, most people think they only have two choices: indulge or repress. If these are the only options, which one looks more "holy"? Repression. Yet there is another way! Rather than repressing lust by pushing it into the subconscious, trying to ignore it, or otherwise seeking to annihilate it, we must *surrender* our lusts to Christ and allow him to "crucify" them. As we do, "the Spirit of the Lord gives new form to our desires" (*CCC*, 2764). As we allow lust to be crucified, we also come to experience the resurrection of God's original plan for eros. Not immediately, but gradually, as we take up our cross every day and follow, we pass through various (and sometimes painful) purifications and, through it all, we come to experience sexual desire as the power to love in God's image.

This process of transformation requires not only a resolute will but also a firm faith. It's the Holy Spirit who transforms our hearts, who reinflates our tires, who fills us with new wine. And faith, you may recall, is the openness of the human heart to God's gift of the Holy Spirit.[52]

When lust tempts you, or even overwhelms you, you might say a prayer like this:

Lord, I thank you for the gift of my sexual desires. I surrender this lustful desire to you and I ask you please, by the power of your death and resurrection, to "untwist" in me what sin has twisted, so that I might come to experience sexual desire as you created it to be—as the desire to love in your image.

Death and Resurrection of Desire

To reinforce your decision to "die" to lust, you may also want to place yourself in the shape of a cross—arms outstretched—while offering the above prayer. The point here is to conform yourself to Christ, to carry "in the body the death of Jesus, so that the life of Jesus may also be manifested in your bodies" (2 Corinthians 4:10).

Resolving *not* to indulge lust can be very difficult, at times even emotionally and physically wrenching. It seems few men and women experience the freedom for which Christ has set us free because when they taste this kind of crucifixion, rather than staying the course that leads to resurrection, they "come down from the cross." When those nails are biting into your hands, and the burden of the cross seems too heavy to bear, keep going! You are on the verge of a passing over from death to life, from lust to authentic love. Only if we are willing to die with Christ can we also live the resurrected life he offers.

The grand storyteller C. S. Lewis shares a powerful image of this death and resurrection at the end of his book *The Great Divorce*. Before a human ghost can enter heaven, he must contend with the vice of lust, symbolized by a red lizard perched on the ghost's shoulder. When the Angel of Fire who guards the eternal gates asks permission to slay the lizard, we can all relate to the ghost's long list of excuses: not today; the gradual process is better; it will hurt too much; it might kill me; let me get an opinion from another doctor, and so on. Weighing the alternatives and realizing it would be better to be dead than to live with this vice, the ghost at long last grants permission. The Angel of Fire immediately grabs the lizard, twists its back, breaks its neck, and flings it to the ground.

As soon as the lizard is slain, the ghost takes on radiant flesh, a resurrected man, and pure love flows out of him "like liquid," says Lewis. But that's not even the best part. The lizard is also resurrected—now transformed into a great white stallion with a tail and mane of gold. The gates of heaven open, the resurrected man mounts the stallion, and redeemed eros itself is what enables him to climb the "impossible steeps" of life everlasting.

"What is a lizard compared with a stallion?" asks Lewis. "Lust is a weak, poor, whimpering, whispering thing compared with the richness and energy of desire which will arise when lust has been killed."[53] When lust has been *killed*. Perhaps we cling to lust in our lives because we're convinced that starvation is the only alternative to the fast food. But if God has prepared a banquet for us, an everlasting wedding feast that satisfies the deepest cry of eros beyond our wildest imaginings, then dying to lust means we *lose nothing* and *gain everything*, while clinging to lust means we *gain nothing* and *lose everything*. It's our choice. Dear God, grant us the grace to choose you!

Discerning the Movements of Our Hearts

Let me emphasize—if this is not clear enough already—that the positive approach to purity I am outlining with John Paul II's help does not provide a license to push the envelope. The person who uses anything in this book as an excuse to indulge his (or her) lusts is not seeking purity. Honest people know their limits. They know what situations would make them stumble and they avoid them with the seriousness Christ demands of us. "If your right eye causes you to sin, pluck it out . . . if your right hand causes you to sin, cut it off" (Matthew 5:29–30). Modern adaptation: "If your iPhone causes you to sin, throw it away. If your laptop causes you to sin, get rid of it."

It's true that sometimes love and lust are difficult to distinguish. A man, for example, upon recognizing a woman's beauty, might wonder where the line is between seeing her as an object for his own gratification and loving her rightly as a person made in God's image. As John Paul II writes, lust "is not always plain and obvious; sometimes it is concealed, so that it passes itself off as 'love.' . . . Does this mean that we should distrust the human heart? No!" he insists. "It is only to say that we must remain in control of it" (TOB 32:3).

"Control" here doesn't mean merely dominating unruly desires in order to keep them in check. Again, that is only the negative side of the picture. As we mature in self-control, we experience it as *"the ability to orient* [sexual] reactions, both as to their content and as to their character" (TOB 129:5). The person who is truly master of himself is able to direct eros "toward what is true, good, and beautiful, so that what is 'erotic' also becomes true, good, and beautiful" (TOB 48:1). As this happens, we come to understand and experience the mystery of sexuality "in a depth, simplicity, and beauty hitherto altogether unknown" (TOB 117b:5).

To paraphrase a very insightful passage, this great pope-saint observes that getting to this point demands "perseverance and consistency" in learning the meaning of our bodies, the meaning of our sexuality. We must learn this not only in the abstract (although this, too, is necessary), but above all in the interior reactions of our own "hearts." This is a "science," John Paul II says, which can't really be learned only from books, because it's a question here of deep knowledge of our interior life. Deep in the heart we learn to distinguish between what, on the one hand, composes the great riches of sexuality and sexual attraction, and what, on the other hand, bears only the sign of lust. And although these internal movements of the heart can sometimes be confused with one another, we have been called by Christ to acquire a mature and complete evaluation. And he concludes, "It should be added that this task *can* be carried out and that it is truly worthy of man" (TOB 48:4).

FOR REFLECTION

1. In what ways do you question God's gift, feeling that he won't give you what you really want?

2. What teachings of the Church feel like a burden or imposition to you? How might God be speaking to you through this?

3. How does purity differ from prudishness? How does lust differ from love?

Lord, help me to discern the movements of my heart.
Help me to distinguish between the great riches of sexuality as you
created it to be and the distortions of lust. I grant you permission,
Lord, to lead me on the journey of full purification from all my lusts.
Take them, Lord. Crucify them so that I might come to experience
the resurrection of sexual desire as you intend. Grant me a pure
heart so that I might see you. Amen.

FOUR

The Resurrection of the Body

"And so we will be with the Lord forever" (1 Thessalonians 4:17)...
"as a bride adorned for her husband" (Revelation 21:2). Here is what awaits
us [in the resurrection]! ... And it is not just a manner of
speaking: they will be real and true nuptials!
—Pope Francis

Allow me to take you with me on the last leg of one of my backpacking trips. I've been trudging through the woods with nearly fifty pounds on my back for several days. Exposure to the elements and restless nights in a tent have taken their toll. I've successfully sidestepped a few coiled rattlesnakes. Slipping on boulders a couple days earlier has scraped up my shins. Every bend of my left knee aggravates a sharp pain in my joint, and each placement of my foot reminds me that my open blisters will take a week to heal. But I'm almost there, and the sure hope of arrival keeps me going . . . one arduous step at a time. The elation of having completed the journey will soon be mine. *I can do this. I'm almost there. Keep going . . .*

In his marvelous letter *Saved in Hope*, Pope Benedict XVI wrote that "the present, even if it is arduous, can be lived and accepted if it leads toward a goal, if we can be sure of this goal, and if the goal is great enough to justify the effort of the journey."⁵⁴ Being human is not easy. The journey toward our destiny is not easy. But Christ gives us assurance of the goal. He also gives us assurance that the sufferings of the journey are *nothing* compared to the glory that awaits us (see Romans 8:18).

All of creation, St. Paul tells us—and this means the entire universe and all it contains—waits "with eager longing" for this glory to be revealed "because the creation itself will be set free from its bondage to decay" (Romans 8:19, 21). We know, in fact, that "all of creation has been groaning as in the pains of childbirth" and that "we ourselves . . . groan inwardly as we wait for . . ." (Romans 8:22–23)—as we wait for *what*? What is it we're waiting for? What is it that we're journeying toward? What *is* this glory, and how great must it be that St. Paul can say it makes all human suffering (from the beginning of time till the end of time) as nothing compared to it?

St. Paul calls this glory, this "everything" we (and all the universe) are waiting for, yearning for, groaning for, laboring in the pangs of childbirth for, "the redemption of our bodies" (Romans 8:23). And it is precisely hope in the redemption *of our bodies* that "saves us" (see Romans 8:24), that gives us a reason to *stay the journey* "even if it is arduous."

In this chapter, with the help of a mystic-saint who caught a glimpse of life "on the other side" and shared it in his TOB, we will seek to paint a picture, as best we can, of the glory that awaits us in the ultimate realization of redemption, when our bodies will be raised in glory, reunited with our souls, and taken into the eternal "wedding feast" (assuming we say "yes" to God's invitation). As St. Paul put it, our goal is to have "the eyes of [our] hearts enlightened," so that we may "know what is the hope" to which we are called, "the riches of his glorious inheritance," and "the immeasurable greatness of his power" at work in us (Ephesians 1:18–19).

In the Resurrection

Christ entered history in "the fullness of time" (Galatians 4:4). In this sense, if Christ is who he says he is (God in the flesh), his time on earth two thousand years ago is the fulcrum of human history. From this fulcrum, Christ wants to reveal to us who we really are, and he does so by pivoting in two directions. *Historical* men and women live in a tension between the two poles of our *origin* and our *destiny* (see TOB 71:2). And this is where Christ calls us to find our true selves: right in this "tension."

In his discussion with the Pharisees about marriage in Matthew 19, Christ pivots toward "the beginning"; in his discussion with the Sadducees about marriage in Matthew 22, Christ pivots toward "the end." In the former, he points us to the state of man and woman's relationship *before* sin. In the latter, he points us to the state of man and woman's relationship *beyond* sin. Returning to our image of the deflated tires, our destiny cannot be understood only as a return to the fully "inflated" state of the beginning. Our destiny introduces us to an entirely *new* dimension of human life, love, sex, gender, and marriage "beyond all understanding and description" (*CCC*, 1027). Tires, you might say, will give way to *flight*.

Christ reveals this *entirely new* dimension of human existence when he says that "in the resurrection they neither marry nor are given in marriage" (Matthew 22:30). This statement is the final of the three key words that John Paul II examines in order to discover a "total vision of man." We will look first at the expression "in the resurrection," and then we will examine what it means that we will not be "given in marriage."

Heaven—A Bodily Experience

At seminars for priests, I often ask them what percentage of their parishioners would they think view their bodies as a shell that they're anxious to shed at death or even as a prison from which they hope to be liberated. The lowest answer I've gotten over the years is about 75 percent. Most say about 95 percent.

Mercy. This is *not* the Christian view of things. Rather, it's a view from the philosophy of Plato that has crept into the minds of many Christians. The truth about man's destiny "cannot be understood as a state of the soul alone, separated (according to Plato, liberated) from the body," St. John Paul II tells us. Instead, Scripture teaches that the afterlife "must be understood as *the definitively and perfectly 'integrated' state of man* brought about by a [perfect] union of the soul with the body" (TOB 66:6).

The *Catechism* observes, "'On no point does the Christian faith meet with more opposition than on the resurrection of the body.' It is very commonly accepted that the life of the human person continues in a spiritual fashion after death. But how can we believe that this body, so clearly mortal, could rise to everlasting life?" (*CCC*, 996). What a mystery! We "await a savior, the Lord Jesus Christ, who will change our mortal bodies to conform to his glorified body" (Philippians 3:20–21). In Christ "the mortal puts on immortality" (1 Corinthians 15:54).

Of course, we often speak of the "souls" in heaven. When we buried my mother-in-law, I saw her body go into the ground, and I am confident that her soul is now enjoying some form of union with God. But the souls currently in heaven ("currently," of course, is a time-bound word that does not even apply to heaven) remain in an in-human state until the resurrection of their bodies. My mother-in-law's body is now returning to dust. But if God can gather up dust and breathe his life into it at the beginning of time, he can certainly do it again at the end of time. Hence, it is misleading to speak only as if the soul is going to live forever. What is proper to Christian faith is to recognize that it is *the person* who is called to eternal life, not merely the *soul* of the person. As St. Bonaventure asserted, "The soul is not a person, but the soul, joined to the body, is a person."[55]

The perfect reunion of body and soul is our only hope as human beings, for that's what we *are* as human beings: the union of body and soul. The separation of the two at death is entirely "unnatural." As Peter Kreeft writes:

> A soul without a body is exactly the opposite of what Plato thought it is. It is not free but bound . . . That is why the resurrection of the body is . . . not a dispensable extra. When death separates the two we have a freak, a monster, an obscenity. That is why we are terrified of ghosts and corpses, though both are harmless: they are the obscenely separated aspects of what belongs together as one."[56]

Divinized and Spiritualized Bodies

Our bodies will certainly be different in their resurrected state (recall that the disciples did not recognize Jesus after the resurrection; see Luke 24:15–16), but we will still have them! The difference is that our bodies will be perfectly "spiritualized" (see

1 Corinthians 15:44). Spiritualization means that *"the powers of the spirit will permeate the energies of the body"* (TOB 67:1). And because the "spirit" that will permeate our bodies is not only our own human, created spirit, but the divine, uncreated Holy Spirit, John Paul II speaks also of the "divinization" (making divine) of the body. In a way inaccessible to us now, we will participate, body and soul, "in the divine nature" (2 Peter 1:4).

Recall our earlier discussion of God's innermost secret: "God himself is an eternal exchange of love, Father, Son, and Holy Spirit, and he has destined us to share in that exchange" (*CCC*, 221). This is what we mean by the "spiritualization" and "divinization" of the body. To the degree that creatures can, we will share—body and soul—in God's eternal exchange of love. And this "great mystery" is prefigured right from the beginning in man and woman's "exchange of love," that is, in and through their union in "one flesh."

Many ask, will there be sex in heaven? It depends what we mean by the term. Sex is not *first* what people *do*. It is who people *are* as male or female. John Paul II mentions several times that we will be raised as male and female (see TOB 66:4). So, in this sense, yes, there will be sex in heaven: We will be fully masculine and fully feminine. But, as we will learn from Christ's words about the resurrection, the union of the sexes as we know it now will give way to an *infinitely greater* union. Those who are raised in glory will experience a bliss so far superior to earthly sexual union that our wee brains cannot even begin to fathom it. Eye has not seen, ear has not heard, nor has it even dawned on us what God has prepared for those who love him (see 1 Corinthians 2:9).

Christ Points Us to the Ultimate "Marriage"

At first glance, Christ's words that we are no longer "given in marriage" may seem to undermine all we have said about the greatness of marital love and the sexual embrace. But examined more closely, these words point to the crowning glory of all we've said. Marriage exists from the beginning to point us to the "marriage of the Lamb" (Revelation 19:7), to the union of Christ and the Church (see Ephesians 5:31–32). These are the real nuptials for which we yearn.

As biblical scholar Dennis Kinlaw puts it, when the Bible speaks of "the New Jerusalem coming down out of heaven 'prepared as a bride beautifully dressed for her husband' (Revelation 21:2) . . . the human story that began with a wedding comes to its end; the wedding in the garden of Eden and every other wedding in human history . . . prefigured this end—a royal wedding—the one in which the Father gives a bride to his Son." This means that marriage was designed by God "to teach human creatures what human history is really all about."[57]

What is human history really all about? Marriage . . . *to God*. This is *why we exist*: to participate in the eternal exchange of love found in God by being wed eternally to his Son. This is why we have that ache inside us. That "something" we're all looking for is the eternal bliss of being one with God. As Pope Francis put it, the eternal marriage of Christ and the Church "is nothing more than the fulfillment of the plan of communion and love woven by God throughout history."[58]

The union of the sexes—as beautiful and wonderful as it is in the divine plan—is only a faint glimmer, a pale picture within time of that eternal union with God. In the resurrection, the "primordial sacrament" will give way to the divine reality. In other words, if God created the union of the sexes as a foreshadowing of heaven, when Christ says that in the resurrection we're no longer given in marriage, he's saying: "You no longer need a foreshadowing to point you *to* heaven when you are *in* heaven. You're there. The ultimate union has come."

People often ask, "Does this mean I won't be with my spouse in heaven?" Assuming both spouses say "yes" to God's wedding invitation, they will certainly be together. All who respond will live together in a communion that fulfills superabundantly all that is true, good, and beautiful about marriage and family life here on earth. What we need to understand is that the union of the sexes is not our be-all and end-all. It's only an icon, a sign of something infinitely greater. Paraphrasing John Paul II, marriage does not express definitively the deepest meaning of sexuality. It merely provides a concrete expression of that meaning within history (see TOB 69:4). At the end of history, the "historical" expression of sexuality will make way for an entirely new expression of our call to life-giving communion.

Icons and Idols

When we lose sight of that infinitely greater union, we inevitably treat the icon as an idol. In other words, when we lose sight of the joys of heaven, we tend to view sexual union and its physical pleasures as our ultimate fulfillment. Welcome to the world in which we live.

Still, there is an important element of truth in our society's idolatrous obsession with sex. Recall that behind every false god, we discover our desire for the true God gone awry. The sexual confusion so prevalent in our world and in our own hearts is actually the human desire for heaven gone berserk. Untwist the distortions, and we discover the astounding glory of sex in the divine plan. "For this reason . . . the two become one flesh." For what reason? To reveal, proclaim, and anticipate the eternal union of Christ and the Church (see Ephesians 5:31–32).

Sin means to "miss the mark." It's an archer's term. So is the word "destiny": It means "to aim at." When we sin, we're actually aiming for something good, but we miss the target. And when that target is heaven, that's a mark we really don't want to miss!

"What does what you're doing *here* have to do with . . . *the stars?*" asked the old priest of the young lovers. Here's the answer: God gave us eros to be like the fuel of a rocket that's meant to launch us to the heavens—"to infinity . . . and beyond!" Yet what would happen if the engines of that rocket became inverted, pointing us back upon ourselves and no longer toward the stars? Launch that rocket, and the result is a massive blast of self-destruction. Herein we discover the importance of Christ's words about the new state of the body and sex in the resurrection: They help us set our sights on the union that alone can satisfy. As we allow the power of these words to sink into our hearts, they begin to redirect our rocket engines toward the stars. In this way, our *desire*, as we embrace our true *design*, points us back to our eternal *destiny* (see my book *Fill These Hearts* for a thorough look at living your life according to these "three Ds"). In turn, the idol once again can become the icon it was meant to be.

This is the *redemption* of desire. We must "not be discouraged by the difficulty or the obstacles that come from sin," wrote Pope Benedict. "In this regard, we must not forget that the dynamism of desire is always open to redemption. . . . We all, moreover, need to set out on the path of purification and healing of desire. We are pilgrims, heading for the heavenly homeland." The pilgrimage of *eros* "is not, then, about suffocating the longing that dwells in the heart of man, but about freeing it, so that it can reach its true height."[59] And its true height is nothing short of infinity!

Only to the degree that eros is aimed toward the stars does marriage take on its true meaning as a sacrament. Sacraments, when properly lived, give us a taste of heaven on earth. But when heaven comes, the sacraments, having served their purpose, give way. There will be no sacraments in heaven (see *CCC*, 671), not because sacraments are annihilated, but because they are superabundantly fulfilled. Hence, the fact that we no longer marry in the resurrection should not cause sadness but rejoicing. Every human longing, every desire of the heart for love and union will be fulfilled beyond our wildest dreams. That deep ache of solitude will finally be completely and eternally satisfied.

Experience attests that even the most wonderful marriage does not fully satisfy our hunger for love and union. We still yearn for something more. I love my wife, Wendy, more than any words can express, but she will not mind my saying that she is not my ultimate fulfillment. We must not hang our hats on a hook that cannot bear the weight! If we look to another human person as our ultimate fulfillment, we will crush that person. Only the eternal, ecstatic marriage of heaven—so far superior to anything proper to earthly life that we cannot begin to fathom it—can satisfy the human ache of solitude.

The Beatific Vision

There are clear and important distinctions to be made regarding our original, historical, and ultimate existences, but there is also a continuity. In short, if our origin and our history revolve around the mystery of divine love and spousal communion, then our heavenly existence will revolve around the same, albeit in an entirely new dimension. Now we see dimly, as in a mirror, but then we will behold the mystery "face-to-face" (see 1 Corinthians 13:12).

"Because of his transcendence, God cannot be seen as he is unless he himself opens up his mystery to man's immediate contemplation and gives him the capacity for it. The Church calls this contemplation of God in his heavenly glory 'the beatific vision'" (CCC, 1028). "Beatify" means to make supremely happy, utterly blissful. The unsurpassed beauty and splendor of the eternal vision of God will fill all who behold with never-ending ecstasy.

Recall man and woman's original face-to-face vision of each other. This provides a faint glimmer or prefiguration of the beatific vision. As John Paul II says, man and woman experienced a "beatifying immunity from shame" in their nakedness precisely because their vision was infused with love. "Happiness is being rooted in love," he affirms (TOB 16:3). Man and woman had no fear of being fully "seen" by the other because each loved and received the other in the full truth of his or her naked humanity. Their mutual vision expressed their profound, personal knowledge of each other. They participated in the sheer goodness of each other's humanity.

John Paul writes that the beatific vision of heaven is "a concentration of knowledge . . . and love on God himself." This knowledge "cannot be anything but full participation in God's inner life, that is, in trinitarian Reality itself" (TOB 68:4). In the beatific vision we will *know* God and he will *know* us (he already does, of course). We will *participate* fully in God's divinity, and he will *participate* fully in our humanity (he already does, of course, having taken on human nature in the Incarnation).

God has humbled himself to share in human life so that we might share in divine life. What a glorious exchange! As the *Catechism* says, the "Son of God became man so that we might become God" (*CCC*, 460), so that we might participate in the divine nature (see 2 Peter 1:4). This, of course, does not mean that we will lose our human nature and become on par with God. It does mean, though, that God will give us a share in his own divinity, to the degree that our humanity will allow.

This divine-human exchange expresses something of the "content" or inner dynamic of the beatific vision. Recall here that this is exactly what the serpent convinced us God was withholding—his divine life and our happiness. "If you want to be 'like God,'" he insinuated "you need to *grasp* at it." No! God has always desired for us to share fully in his own divinity. It is a free gift! All we need do is open to *receive* it. We need not grasp at what God freely gives us. Sin—and all human misery—begins right here, with grasping at the gift.

Fulfillment of the Spousal Meaning of the Body
How will this glorious exchange between God and man take place? Since the nuptials of heaven are beyond all human knowledge, all we can do is speculate. Yet once again we see a faint glimmer of what is to come in the nuptials of earth.

The original exchange of man and woman took place through the "freedom of the gift" and the "spousal meaning of the body."

Recall that God gave us freedom as the capacity to love, as the capacity to make a sincere gift of ourselves to one another. "Man can only find himself through the sincere gift of self."[60] Furthermore, God inscribed this call to self-donation right in our bodies as male and female. Our bodies have a spousal meaning because they are capable of expressing divine love, *"precisely that love in which the person becomes a gift* and—through this gift—fulfills the very meaning of his being and existence" (TOB 15:1).

Paraphrasing John Paul II, in the resurrection we discover—in a new, heavenly dimension—the same spousal meaning of the body. This time, however, the spousal meaning of the body is fulfilled in our meeting with the mystery of the living God, through our vision of him face-to-face (see TOB 67:5). Applying the spousal analogy, we can conclude that in the resurrection, the divine Bridegroom will express his gift ("This is my body given for you") in its fullest reality. All who respond to the wedding invitation will open to receive this gift as Christ's Bride. In response to this gift, we will give ourselves totally to the divine Bridegroom in an eternally life-giving embrace.

As the *Catechism* states, the Church "longs to be united with Christ, her Bridegroom, in the glory of heaven," where she "will rejoice one day with [her] Beloved, in a happiness and rapture that can never end" (*CCC*, 1821). John Paul II writes that in this heavenly reality "penetration and permeation of what is essentially human by what is essentially divine will then reach its peak" (TOB 67:3).

The erotic imagery is unmistakable. It may be rather scandalous to some, but this imagery has deep biblical roots. God loves as a

Bridegroom, as "a lover with all the passion of a true love," says Pope Benedict. Indeed, the biblical prophets of old "described God's passion for his people using boldly erotic images."[61] Of course, when using erotic love as an image of heaven, it's especially important to remember the inadequacy of analogies. Heaven is not some eternally magnified experience of sexual union on earth. As John Paul II observes, the union to come "will be a completely new experience." Yet "at the same time," he says, "it will not be alienated in any way" from the love that man and woman experienced in the beginning and have sought to reclaim throughout history (see TOB 69:5).

In the resurrection we will experience the ultimate fulfillment of the "redemption of our bodies" (Romans 8:23). The original meaning of the body will then be revealed again in such *simplicity and splendor*, when all who respond to the wedding invitation will live in the full freedom of self-giving love (see TOB 69:6). Those whose bodies rise to eternal life will experience "the absolute and eternal spousal meaning of the glorified body . . . in union with God himself" (TOB 75:1).

The Communion of Saints

We will live this self-giving love not only as individuals in union with God. As alluded to earlier, we will also live in self-giving love and communion with all the saints who enjoy the beatific vision. Recall that, in his experience of solitude, Adam discovered his fundamental vocation: love of God *and* love of neighbor. Heaven fulfills both dimensions of this vocation. When we reach our ultimate destiny we will live in consummate union with all who are raised in glory.

"*For man*, this consummation will be the final realization of the unity of the human race, which God willed from creation . . . Those who are united with Christ will form the community of the redeemed, 'the holy city' of God, 'the Bride, the wife of the Lamb'" (*CCC*, 1045). What was "the unity of the human race, which God willed from creation"? It was the unity of the two, male and female, in "one body" (Genesis 2:24). In the communion of saints there are "many parts" (a great multitude of glorified men and women), yet all are united eternally in "one body" (see 1 Corinthians 12:20).

This obviously will not be experienced in the sexual sense lived here on earth. Yet we can conclude that, in some mysterious way beyond earthly comprehension, all that is masculine in our humanity will be in union with all that is feminine in our humanity. That unity—that "one body"—will be the one Bride of Christ living in consummate union with her Bridegroom forever. In and through this communion with Christ, the communion of saints will live in communion with *the* Communion, the Trinity. We will *see* all and *be seen* by all. We will *know* all and *be known* by all—and God will be "all in all" (Ephesians 1:23).

As if it needs to be said again, *this* is the purpose of sexual union in the divine plan: to prefigure in some way the glory, ecstasy, and bliss that awaits us in heaven (see Ephesians 5:31–32). As the *Catechism* expresses it, "In the joys of their love [God gives spouses] here on earth a foretaste of the wedding feast of the Lamb" (*CCC*, 1642). And recall Pope Benedict's glorious proclamation that eros is meant "to provide not just fleeting pleasure, but a certain foretaste of the pinnacle of our existence, of that beatitude for which our whole being yearns."[62]

No wonder we are all so interested in sex. God put an innate desire in every human being to want to understand the meaning of our creation as male and female and our call to union. Why? To lead us to him. But beware of the counterfeits! Because sex is meant to launch us toward heaven, the enemy attacks *right there*. When our God-given curiosity about sex is not met with the "great mystery" of the divine plan, we inevitably fall, in one way or another, for the counterplan. In other words, when our desire to understand the body and sexuality is not met with the truth, we inevitably fall for the lies.

Our God Is Rich in Mercy

If what you're discovering about God's banquet through the TOB is news to you, chances are you've either built a life around starving eros or indulging it in fast food. Or, if you're like me, you've oscillated between the two. Either approach leaves us wounded and deeply in need of God's mercy.

Mercy. The Latin, *misericordia*, means "a heart which gives itself to those in misery." And whether we've opted for a starvation diet or fast food, both lead to misery; both separate us from God. Listen to this powerful invitation from Pope Francis:

> Now is the time to say to Jesus: "Lord, I have let myself be deceived; in a thousand ways I have shunned your love, yet here I am once more, to renew my covenant with you. I need you. Save me once again, Lord, take me once more into your redeeming embrace."[63]

If you've taken a repressive approach to desire, then you might add to the above prayer with something like this:

Lord, I have been afraid of my desire. I have been afraid that living from that "fire" inside me would only cause me pain or lead me astray. Awaken a holy and noble eros in me, Lord. Give me the courage to feel it and help me to experience it as my desire for your Fire. Help me also to rejoice rightly in the many gifts and pleasures of this life as so many signs of the joy that awaits me in heaven. Amen.

If you've taken an indulgent approach to desire, you might want to pray like this:

Lord, I have taken my desire to things that cannot satisfy. I have not known how to remain in my ache for you, how to wait on you, how to trust in you . . . so I have grasped at a great many pleasures apart from you. Please help me redirect my desire from the finite pleasures of this world to the infinite ecstasy that awaits me in heaven, and help me to recognize all the good things you have made in this world as so many icons pointing me to you. Amen.

Why was Christ so compassionate toward sexual sinners, especially women? Can we not recognize that, behind their deception, he knew they were looking for him, the true Bridegroom?

Think of the woman caught in adultery (see John 8:2–11). She went looking for love, intimacy, union with another, but, as always, the counterfeit couldn't satisfy. Laden with shame, she was brought before Christ by an angry crowd anxious to stone her. Christ then said whoever was without sin could cast the first stone. According to his own words, the sinless Christ could have thrown a stone, but Christ came not to condemn. He came to save (see John 3:17).

St. John writes that "Jesus was left alone with the woman standing before him" (John 8:9). Reading into the story a bit, we can imagine that in the woman's encounter with the divine Bridegroom, she had a conversion from the counterfeit to the real thing. Do you think when Jesus said, "Go, and do not sin again" (John 8:11), that she turned and grumbled, "Who is this man to tell me what I can and cannot do with my body!"? Or do you think, having encountered the love she was truly looking for, she left transformed, renewed, affirmed in the deepest part of her being as a woman?

What are the lies you have believed about your body, about the bodies of others, about the meaning of gender and sexuality? What are the counterfeits you have accepted as reality? What are the wounds you've endured because of your own folly and the folly of others? Behind all the pain and all the distortions is your authentic thirst for the eternal joys of heaven. Sexual sin is a quest to satisfy that thirst with "dead water." Christ meets us right there without condemnation: "If you knew the gift of God . . . you would have asked him and he would have given you living water" (John 4:10). But, like so many of us, the "woman at the well" didn't know the gift of God, so she had taken her thirst elsewhere: "You have had five husbands, and he whom you now have is not your husband" (John 4:18). Six lovers. Do you see the symbolism? Six is the imperfect biblical number. Seven is the perfect biblical number. Who is this woman's "seventh lover"? Christ, the Bridegroom! His love is what she's been thirsting for the whole time—a "living water" welling up to eternal life (see John 4:1–36).

How tender Jesus is with our broken humanity! We must not fear to throw our wounded sexuality wide open to Christ, to invite his healing, merciful love to come in to all of our diseased images and painful memories, so that he can touch our wounds. Christ *never* robs us of our humanity. He restores it to us. He comes not to impose rules upon us, but to teach us tenderly the ways of authentic love. "Being Christian is not the result of an ethical choice or a lofty idea," insists Pope Benedict, "but the encounter with . . . a person, which gives life a new horizon and a decisive direction."[64] That decisive direction is precisely the journey toward heaven, toward the full experience of love and "the redemption of our bodies."

This is "a journey totally sustained by grace," John Paul II tells us. It also "demands an intense spiritual commitment and is no stranger to painful purifications."[65] But, like the challenge of a backpacking trip, if we keep putting one foot in front of the other, we'll make it to our destiny. Life, "even if it is arduous, can be lived and accepted if it leads toward a goal, if we can be sure of this goal, and if the goal is great enough to justify the effort of the journey."[66] What's the goal that justifies all the trials, struggles, and sufferings of this life? Where does this crazy journey lead? To being "wholly possessed by the divine Beloved," John Paul II tells us, "to the ineffable joy experienced by the mystics as 'nuptial union'"[67]—to eternal ecstasy, unrivaled rapture, bounteous, beauteous bliss.

FOR REFLECTION

————————

1. Do you view your body as a shell you're eager to shed at death—or even a prison from which you hope to be liberated? Where do you think these ideas come from?

2. What are some lies you have believed about your body, about the bodies of others, about the meaning of gender and sexuality? What are the counterfeits you have accepted as reality?

3. What wounds have you endured because of your own unwise actions and/or the wrongful actions of others?

Lord, grant me faith. Help me believe in the glorious gift of the resurrection of the body lived in the nuptials of eternity. Help me to turn to you and allow you to quench my authentic thirst for these eternal joys. And help me stay the journey, come what may. Amen.

FIVE

Celibacy for the Kingdom

---

*Celibacy for the kingdom signifies the risen man, in [whom] the
absolute and eternal spousal meaning of the glorified body will be
revealed in union with God himself.*

—St. John Paul II

Let's return to the scene of the elderly monsignor interrupting the
young couple under the stars. It's quite a picture—two passionate
lovers and a celibate priest looking up at the heavens together. The
lovers hearken back to God's original plan for man and woman,
and the celibate priest hearkens forward to the ultimate plan when
eros will find superabundant fulfillment in the nuptials of eternity.
Both need each other. The couple needs the celibate witness to help
direct their love toward the stars, and those who are consecrated
celibates need the love of man and woman to keep them grounded
in the spousal meaning of their own bodies.

As we continue our exploration of the TOB, we will see clearly
how both vocations provide a "full answer," John Paul II tells us,
to the "question about the meaning of 'being a body,' that is, the
meaning of masculinity and femininity, of being . . . a man or a
woman" (TOB 85:9).

The Meaning of Being Human

We have looked in the last three chapters at our origin, history, and destiny in order to answer the question "What does it mean to be human?" So, what *does* it mean? In brief, we have learned that to be human means we are called to *communion*—communion with God and with one another in a rapture and bliss that will never end. This means that "we are in the middle of a love story," says Pope Francis, "each of us is a link in this chain of love. And if we do not understand this, we have understood nothing of what the Church is."[68]

We've also learned throughout that our bodies tell this love story, that this call to communion with God and with all humanity is *stamped right in our bodies* as male and female. Eros was given to us by God precisely to lead us to the eternal marriage of Christ and the Church. What typically passes for Christianity in the modern world—a list of oppressive rules aimed precisely at squelching eros—couldn't be further from what Christianity actually is. It's an invitation to the ultimate satisfaction of eros in an eternal communion beyond our wildest imaginings.

As we come to realize *who we really are* as male and female, we also come to realize *how we are to live.* We come to realize that love is "the fundamental and innate vocation of every human being." And we come to realize that there are "two specific ways of realizing the vocation of the human person, in its entirety, to love: marriage and virginity or celibacy. Either one is in its own proper form an actuation of the most profound truth about man, of his being 'created in the image of God.'"[69]

Subsequent chapters are dedicated to the sacrament of

marriage, while this chapter will explore the celibate life.[70] St. John Paul II begins here because, as we will see, we can't know what marriage is a sacrament *of* unless we first understand Christian celibacy. This chapter will also prove meaningful for those who are single and might prefer not to be. As John Paul II observed, a proper understanding of Christian celibacy can "enlighten and help those who, for reasons independent of their own will, have been unable to marry and have then accepted their situation in a spirit of service."[71]

A growing number of men and women find themselves single and would very much prefer not to be. I have great reverence for that cry of the heart for a spouse. I know how agonizing it can be both from my own experience in life and from the honor of having many single people over the years share their hearts with me. We all experience that ache of solitude and long for it to be filled. However, that longing "is not finally and completely satisfied simply by union with another human being," as John Paul II rightly observed.[72] In fact, if eros is truly a cry of our hearts for the infinite, then the marriage we really desire is the one already promised us: the marriage of the Lamb.

Whether we are single, married, or consecrated celibates, setting our sights on that eternal union is the only hope that can safely see us through the inevitable sorrows and trials of this life. "Then you shall see and be radiant, your heart shall thrill and rejoice" (Isaiah 60:5). Never again will you hunger; never again will you thirst. For the Bridegroom will lead you to springs of living water and wipe away every tear from your eyes (see Revelation 7:16–17). Witnessing to this *living hope* is the very essence of Christian celibacy.

Eunuchs for the Kingdom

When Jesus restored the permanence of marriage according to God's original plan, his disciples (like many today) concluded that it was better not to marry at all (see Matthew 19:10). In response to their contention, Jesus takes the discussion to a different plane altogether: "For there are eunuchs who have been so from birth, and there are eunuchs who have been made eunuchs by men, and there are eunuchs who have made themselves eunuchs for the sake of the kingdom of heaven" (Matthew 19:12).

A eunuch is someone physically incapable of sexual relations. In the Christian tradition, a eunuch "for the kingdom of heaven" is someone who freely forgoes sexual relations in anticipation of that state in which men and women "neither marry nor are given in marriage." Celibacy for the kingdom, therefore, "is a sign that the body, whose end is not the grave, is directed to glorification." It "is a testimony among men that anticipates the future resurrection" (TOB 75:1). In a sense, the celibate man or woman steps beyond the dimensions of history—while living within the dimensions of history—and proclaims to the world that "the kingdom of God is here"; the ultimate marriage has come.

Christian celibacy, therefore, is not a rejection of sexuality. It points us to the ultimate purpose and meaning of sexuality. "For this reason . . . the two become one flesh." What reason does St. Paul give? Man and woman become one flesh as a sign or "sacrament" of Christ's eternal union with the Church (see Ephesians 5:31–32). Those who remain celibate for the kingdom forgo the sacrament of marriage in anticipation of the heavenly reality, the marriage of the Lamb. If it is "not good for man to be alone," Christian celibacy reveals that the ultimate fulfillment of solitude is found only in union with God. In a way, the celibate person freely chooses to remain in the ache of solitude in this life in order to devote all of his longings to the union that alone can satisfy.

The word *celibacy*, unfortunately, does not usually carry this profound "spousal" meaning for people. It's a negative word in the sense that it tells us what these people are *not* doing. "Eunuch" can have even worse connotations. Perhaps we would do better to define this vocation in terms of what it embraces and anticipates rather than what it gives up. It embraces and anticipates the heavenly marriage. All people, of course, regardless of their particular vocation, are called to "prepare and perfect themselves for eternal union with God," wrote John Paul II. Christian celibacy, as "the self-giving of a human person wedded to God himself, expressly anticipates this eternal union with God and points the way to it."[73]

Celibacy Must Be Freely Chosen

A survey recently circulated among priests posed a question something like this: "Should celibacy be a free choice or should it continue to be imposed by the Church?" Contrary to widespread opinion, the Church forces *no one* to be celibate. Christ's words ("there are eunuchs who have *made themselves* eunuchs") clearly indicate the importance of the personal choice of this vocation (see TOB 74:1). If someone were *forced* into celibacy, it would be no more legitimate than if someone were *forced* into marriage.

We tend to forget in the Latin Church that male celibacy is a vocation in itself, apart from the priesthood. The Catholic and

Orthodox Churches of the East not only have a valid married priesthood, they also have a vibrant non-ordained celibate brotherhood (this exists in the West as well, but isn't as prominent). As the *Catechism* indicates, the Latin Church usually chooses her priests from among men of faith who have chosen celibacy as their life's vocation (see *CCC*, 1579). This seems to imply that the choice of celibacy should come first. If a Catholic man has discerned a celibate vocation, then, within his life of celibacy, he might also discern a call to priesthood. Those priests who believe celibacy was foisted on them, it seems, have not understood these important distinctions.

As a result, many today are clamoring for an end to priestly celibacy. Some even blame celibacy itself for the sexual problems and abuses of some of the clergy. As I wrote in my book *Good News about Sex & Marriage*, "Celibacy does not *cause* sexual disorder. Sin does. Simply getting married does not *cure* sexual disorder. Christ does. If a priest, or any other man, were to enter marriage with deep-seated sexual disorders, he would be condemning his wife to a life of sexual objectification. The only way the scandal of sexual sin (whether committed by priests or others) will end is if people experience the redemption of their sexuality in Christ."[74]

Authentic Christian celibacy witnesses dramatically to this redemption. It's true that, as a *discipline* of the Latin Church (rather than a *doctrine*), the practice of reserving priestly ordination to those men who have chosen a celibate life could change. But when we realize how celibacy points us to the ultimate meaning of sex, we recognize that our world needs the witness of Christian celibacy now more than ever.

Celibacy Flows from the Redemption of Sexuality

To a world bound by lust, lifelong celibacy seems absurd. The world's general attitude toward Christian celibacy might be summarized like this: "Hey, marriage is the only 'legitimate' chance you Christians get to indulge your lusts. Why the heck would you ever want to give that up? You would be condemning yourself to a life of hopeless repression." But recall that indulgence and repression are not the only choices. There is another way to live the gift of sexuality unknown to the world (and sadly, unknown to many Christians as well). It's the way of redeeming eros.

The difference between marriage and celibacy must *never* be understood as the difference between having a "legitimate" outlet for sexual lust on the one hand and having to repress it on the other. Christ calls *everyone*—no matter his or her particular vocation—to experience redemption from the domination of lust. Only from this perspective do the Christian vocations (celibacy *and* marriage) make any sense. Both vocations—if they are to be lived as Christ intends—should flow from the experience of the redemption of the body.

As John Paul II states, the celibate person must submit *"the sinfulness of his humanity to the powers that flow from the mystery of the redemption of the body . . . just as every other person does"* (TOB 77:4). This is why he indicates that the call to celibacy is not only a matter of formation but of *transformation* (see TOB 81:5). To the degree that a person lives this transformation, he is not bound to indulge libido. He is free with the freedom of the gift. For such a person, sacrificing sexual union (the icon) for the sake of the kingdom (the reality to which the icon points) not only becomes a possibility, it becomes quite attractive. The reality, in fact, is infinitely more attractive than the icon! To think otherwise turns heaven and earth upside down; it turns the icon into an idol.

Addressing consecrated celibates on the role of eros in their vocation, Father Raniero Cantalamessa observed that Christian celibacy witnesses to the truth that "the primary object of our eros, of our search, desire, attraction, passion, must be Christ." He continued:

> Only this is able to defend our heart from going off the rails . . . His love does not subtract us . . . from the attraction of the other sex (this is part of our nature that he has created and does not wish to destroy); he gives us, however, the strength to overcome these attractions with a much stronger attraction. "The chaste one," writes Saint John Climacus, "is he who drives out eros with Eros."[75]

Ah, capital "E" Eros—the very *fire* of God's love—this is where small "e" eros, the fire within each of us—is meant to lead. And if describing God's love with the Greek word *agape* is more familiar to us, recall Pope Benedict XVI's statement that God's love "may certainly be called *eros*." In Christ, *eros* is "supremely ennobled . . . so purified as to become one with *agape*."[76] Indeed, the unification of eros and agape is the "fire" that Christ came to cast upon the earth (see Luke 12:49). (See my book *The Love That Satisfies* for an extended reflection on the unification of eros and agape.)

St. Paul's Teaching

In this context, it's important to understand properly St. Paul's teaching about marriage and celibacy in 1 Corinthians 7. He writes that people who "cannot exercise self-control . . . should marry. For it is better to marry than to be aflame with passion" (v. 9). Is marriage only intended for those who "can't handle" celibacy? Does marriage suddenly make a person's lack of self-control (lust) "okay"? Not according to John Paul II.

The Polish saint reminds us that we cannot interpret Paul's words apart from Christ's words about lust. The verb translated "to be aflame" signifies lust. "To marry" signifies the ethical order—the call to overcome lust—that St. Paul consciously introduces in this context (see TOB 101:3). So, according to John Paul II, it seems that Paul is saying something like this: "It is better to overcome lust through the grace of marriage than to remain engulfed by its flames."

John Paul II acknowledges that Paul's teaching on marriage and celibacy is marked by "his own tone, in some sense, his own 'personal' interpretation" (TOB 82:1). He even asks if Paul's statements indicate a "personal aversion" to marriage (see TOB 83:3). When taken out of context, verses such as "It is well for a man not to touch a woman" (v. 1), "I wish that all were [celibate] as I myself am" (v. 7), and "Do not seek marriage" (v. 27) might lead one to believe so. But John Paul II demonstrates that a thoughtful reading of the whole text leads to a different conclusion.

St. Paul directly combats the badly mistaken idea circulating in Corinth that marriage and sexual union are sinful. Marriage is a "special gift from God" (v. 7). Spouses "should not refuse one another" in their sexual relationship "except perhaps by agreement" (v. 5). And St. Paul commends those who marry for "doing well" (see v. 38).

Is Celibacy "Better" Than Marriage?

Why, then, does St. Paul say that "he who refrains from marriage will do better" than those who marry (v. 38)? Based on these words, the Church has traditionally taught that celibacy is an objectively "superior" vocation. But this must be understood with great care lest we fall into serious error. Many have erroneously concluded that if celibacy is so good, marriage must be so bad. If refraining from sex makes one "pure and holy," having sex—even in marriage—must make one "tainted and dirty." This is *not* the mind of the Church! Such devaluations of marriage and sexual union actually stem from the Manichaean heresy we spoke of earlier.

John Paul II makes it perfectly clear: The "superiority" of celibacy to marriage in the authentic Tradition of the Church "never means disparagement of marriage or belittlement of its essential value. It does not . . . mean a shift, even implicit, on the Manichaean positions, or a support of ways of evaluating or acting based on the Manichaean understanding of the body and sexuality." In the authentic teaching of the Church "we do not find any basis whatsoever for the disparagement of marriage" (TOB 77:6).

Celibacy is the "exceptional" calling because marriage remains the "normal" calling in this life. It is "better" not because of celibacy itself, but because it is chosen *for the kingdom*. It is better in the sense that the heavenly marriage (to which celibates devote themselves more directly) is superior to the earthly marriage. Christian celibacy gives those who live it authentically an even more intense foretaste of the communion to come with God and with all the saints.

Does this mean that if we *really* wanted to follow God, we would all be celibates? No. As St. Paul writes, "Each has his own special gift from God, one of one kind and one of another" (v. 7). We must carefully and prayerfully discern which "gift" God has given us. Subjectively speaking, the better vocation is the one God calls us to as our own personal gift. If marriage is your gift, rejoice! This is your path to heaven. If celibacy is your gift, rejoice! This is your path to heaven.

Marriage and Celibacy Complement Each Other

Marriage and celibacy obviously differ in important ways. Yet these differences do not conflict. The values of one and the other vocation interpenetrate. In fact, marriage and celibacy "explain or complete each other" (TOB 78:2). Marriage reveals the spousal nature of the celibate vocation just as the celibate vocation reveals the great value of marital union. Let me explain.

How does marital love shed light on the nature of the celibate vocation? John Paul II writes that the fidelity and "total self-donation" lived by spouses provide a model for the fidelity and self-donation required of those who choose the celibate vocation. Both vocations in their own way express marital or spousal love, which entails "the complete gift of self" (see TOB 78:4). Furthermore, the fruit of children in married life helps celibate men and women realize that they are called to a fruitfulness as well—a fruitfulness of the spirit. In these ways we see how the "natural" reality of marriage points us to the "supernatural" reality of celibacy for the kingdom. In fact, full knowledge and appreciation of God's plan for marriage and family life are indispensable for the celibate person. As John Paul II expresses it, in order for the celibate person "to be fully aware of *what he is choosing* . . . he must also be fully aware of *what he is renouncing*" (TOB 81:2).

Celibacy, in turn, "has a particular importance and particular eloquence for those who live a conjugal life" (TOB 78:2). As a direct anticipation of the marriage to come, celibacy shows couples what their union is a sacrament *of* by showing them that to which their marriage points. In this way, as Pope Francis expressed, Christian celibacy "encourages married couples to live their own conjugal love against the backdrop of Christ's definitive love, journeying together towards the fullness of the Kingdom."[77]

Furthermore, by abstaining from sexual union, celibates demonstrate the great value of sexual union. How so? A sacrifice only has value to the degree that the thing sacrificed has value. For example, if I were to give up pickles for Lent, there would be no value in that for me, because I do not like pickles. However, if I were to give up beer for Lent, that would be a real sacrifice because I love a good beer. The Church values celibacy so highly *precisely* because she values what it sacrifices—sexual union and all that is connected to it—so highly.

Once again, the self-denial involved in such a sacrifice must not be conceived of as a repression of sexuality. Celibacy for the kingdom is meant to be a fruitful living out of the redemption of sexual desire, understood as the desire to make of oneself a "sincere gift" for others.

Celibacy Expresses the Spousal Meaning of the Body

As we can see, marriage and celibacy are much more closely related than most people realize. Both vocations provide "a full answer" to the meaning of sexuality (see TOB 85:9). That meaning is self-donation in the image of God. As a result, it shouldn't surprise us that whenever a culture devalues sexuality, it inevitably devalues both marriage *and* the celibate vocation. The sexual revolution of the twentieth century has certainly demonstrated this in practice.

John Paul II insists that the celibate life Christ spoke of must flow from a deep and mature awareness of the spousal meaning of the body. Only on this basis does celibacy for the kingdom "find a full guarantee and motivation" (TOB 80:5). Thus, if someone were to choose this vocation based on a fear or rejection of sex, or because of deep-seated sexual wounds that prevented a healthy married life, it would not correspond to Christ's invitation (see TOB 80:7).

If we reject the spousal meaning of our bodies, we do violence to the image of God inscribed in our humanity as male and female. The spousal meaning of the body is "the fundamental component of human existence in the world" (TOB 15:5). It reveals that the human person is created to be a gift "for" another. Christ's words about celibacy show that this "for," which stands at the basis of marriage, can also stand at the basis of celibacy "for" the kingdom of heaven. Therefore, on the basis of the same spousal meaning of the body, there can be formed the love that commits a person to marriage, but there can be formed also the love that commits a person to celibacy "for the kingdom of heaven" (see TOB 80:6).

The point is that our sexuality calls us to give ourselves away in life-giving love. The celibate person doesn't reject this call. He just lives it in a different way. Every man, by virtue of the spousal meaning of his body, is called in some way to be both a husband and a father. Every woman, by virtue of the spousal meaning of her body, is called in some way to be both a wife and a mother. As an image of Christ, the celibate man "marries" the Church. Through his bodily gift of self, he bears numerous "spiritual children." As an image of the Church, the celibate woman "marries" Christ. Through her bodily gift of self, she bears numerous "spiritual children." This is why the terms husband, father, brother, son, and wife, mother, sister, daughter are applicable both to marriage and family life *and* to those who choose celibacy for the kingdom.

The Celibate Marriage of Joseph and Mary

We will conclude our discussion of celibacy by looking briefly at the "oddity" of the virginal marriage of Mary and Joseph. The Catholic Church teaches that Mary and Joseph were given the exceptional calling to embrace both the celibate vocation and the marital vocation *at the same time.* In other words, they lived the earthly marriage and the heavenly marriage simultaneously. In turn, their virginal marriage played an indispensable role in the marriage of heaven and earth: the Word made flesh (see TOB 75:3). In this way Joseph and Mary "became the first witnesses of a fruitfulness different from that of the flesh, that is, the fruitfulness of the Spirit: 'What is begotten in her comes from the Holy Spirit' (Matthew 1:20)" (TOB 75:2).

Joseph and Mary remained virgins not because "sex is bad." As a married couple, they were given the exceptional calling to live their sexuality according to its ultimate meaning—total openness and self-donation to God. By embracing that heavenly dimension of sexuality on earth, they enabled heaven to penetrate earth. As we have been unfolding throughout this book, sexual union, from the beginning, was meant to foreshadow the union of God and man, Christ and the Church. Undoing Eve's "no," Mary, the new Eve, represents the whole human race in giving her "yes" to God's marriage proposal (see *CCC*, 411, 505). Even during her journey on earth, Mary was already participating uniquely in the nuptials of heaven. For her to engage in the sexual act would have been for her a step *backward*. Instead, she pulled Joseph *forward* into the virginal mystery of union with God.

If the Church holds out the Holy Family as a model for all families, this does not imply that married couples should never have sex. Joseph and Mary are a model for all married couples because of their example of total self-donation. The normal call is for spouses to model the Holy Family by living their one-flesh union in total self-donation. In this way, spouses also bring Christ to the world because the marital embrace—when lived as God intends—proclaims the mystery of Christ (see Ephesians 5:31–32).

We will unfold the way in which the one-flesh union proclaims the mystery of Christ more precisely in the next chapter.

FOR REFLECTION

1. What is the ultimate purpose and meaning of sexuality? How can Christian celibacy point us to that ultimate purpose and meaning?

2. Explain why true Christian celibacy should never be understood as a repression of human sexuality.

3. How do marriage and celibacy complement each other? How do they both fulfill the high calling of giving oneself in love to others?

Dear God, whether you call us to marriage or celibacy, help us to give ourselves wholly to you first of all, and then to each other as a self-gift. Teach us how to direct our erotic desires according to your design so we are aimed at our true destiny— eternal union with you. Amen.

SIX

Marriage as a Divine Gift

A man leaves his parents, who gave him life, and is joined to his wife, and one flesh—father, mother, and child—results from the commingling of the two. . . . Our relationship to Christ is similar; we become one flesh with him through communion . . . [and] this has been his plan from the beginning.
—St. John Chrysostom

I remember how excited I was in the fall of 2004 to return from a New York City business trip to tell Wendy what just happened. The biggest publishing house in the world had just offered me a really attractive book deal. They wanted me to write a book for husbands called *Loving Her Rightly*.

Expecting her to rejoice with me at this great opportunity, I was rather stunned when her face immediately fell upon hearing the title of the book. "What's wrong?" I wondered aloud.

Wendy responded, "You and I need to talk . . . and it's gonna be long and it's gonna be painful."

"Whaddaya mean?" I bewilderedly asked.

"Lemme just put it to you this way," she said. "You are in *no place* to be writing a book for husbands called *Loving Her Rightly!*"

To say that exchange was a major wake-up call would be an understatement. For several months, I arranged to have someone watch the kids once a week so we could have time to talk. Actually, for the most part, Wendy talked and I just listened. It was time for me to hear from my wife what ten years of being married to the "Theology of the Body guy" had been like. She was right: It was *long* and it was *painful*. Amid plenty of "wheat" in our relationship, there were also lots of "weeds," and instead of tending to them, I had been traveling the world telling other people about the TOB. Not good.

When I got married in 1995, I had already been studying and sharing the TOB with others for two years. Married life has taught me that it's one thing to have lots of good theology *about* God's plan for man and woman in your head. It's another thing to *live* it. It's one thing to write books, give lectures, and teach classes on the TOB, it's another thing to walk through the "painful purifications" St. John Paul II speaks of that are an absolutely necessary part of the journey. Praise God for his mercy, and for my wife's!

First Ingredient for a Successful Marriage

It's the number one ingredient for a successful marriage: mercy. We must keep this in mind as we venture into this section of John Paul II's teaching. Here, he will be holding out to us the full glory of what God intends for man and woman's relationship. In fact, he insists that if we choose marriage as our vocation, we "must choose it exactly as it was instituted by the Creator 'from the beginning'" (TOB 79:6).

As we've already seen, the original divine plan for marriage *is* glorious. But all of us "fall short of the glory," as St. Paul tells us (see Romans 3:23). All of us must contend with a host of sinful tendencies, not to mention faults, failings, and weaknesses. In light of this, is it even possible for couples to reclaim the original splendor of God's plan?

The *Catechism* responds: "By coming to restore the original order of creation disturbed by sin, [Christ] himself gives the strength and grace to live marriage in the new dimension of the Reign of God." Therefore, "by following Christ, renouncing themselves, and taking up their crosses . . . spouses will be able to 'receive' the original meaning of marriage and live it with the help of Christ" (*CCC*, 1615). As we will see more clearly as we continue, marriage, as a sacrament, plunges spouses right into the heart of the mystery of Christ: the mystery through which we discover that God's grace is sufficient for us, for his power is made perfect in our weakness (see 2 Corinthians 12:9). And this means that there "is no need to be dismayed if love sometimes follows torturous ways. Grace has power to make straight the paths of human love."[78]

The Sacrament

In this chapter, we begin unfolding the section of John Paul II's teaching that he calls "The Sacrament." Marriage, like every other sacrament, has both a divine and a human dimension. The *divine dimension*, which we'll look at here, refers to the heavenly gift God lavishes on us in the sacrament. The *human dimension*, which we'll unfold in the next chapter, refers to the physical sign through which God communicates his gift.

We see the human dimension in the first half of this key statement from Ephesians and divine dimension in the second: "'For this reason a man shall leave his father and mother and be joined to his wife, and the two shall become one flesh.' This is a great mystery, and I mean in reference to Christ and the Church" (Ephesians 5:31–32). Through the human dimension of their union, spouses are caught up into the divine dimension of God's covenant love for humanity, Christ's union with the Church. By calling this section of his TOB "The Sacrament," John Paul II gives us some insight into the relationship of these two unions (husband-wife and Christ-Church). "The Sacrament" obviously refers to marriage, but marriage isn't just about marriage. Marriage, properly understood, extends to something so broad that it "embraces the universe" (TOB 102:8). Marriage as "The Sacrament" refers to the way in which God's eternal mystery "has *become visible* and thereby *entered into the sphere of the Sign*" (TOB 95b:6). And, as such, marriage, right from the beginning, prepared the way for God's wedding himself to us in "one flesh."

In the beginning, God's mystery became visible through the original sign of man's union with woman. In the "fullness of time," this same mystery became visible through the new sign of Christ's union with the Church (see TOB 97:4). As we will come to understand more deeply in this chapter, the "great mystery" is found precisely in the fact that these two signs have become *one*. These two great signs—the union of husband-wife and the union of Christ-Church—express *one mystery* and, thus, form one great sacrament: "*The* Sacrament" (see TOB 95b:7). All of this is contained, as we shall see, in the marvelous teaching of Saint Paul in Ephesians 5.

Crowning of All the Themes in Scripture

As we said in chapter one, it is virtually impossible to overstate how important Ephesians 5 is for John Paul II. He sees in this passage the "crowning" of all the themes in Sacred Scripture—the "central reality" of the whole of divine revelation (see TOB 87:3). In fact, he believes that Ephesians 5 contains what God "wishes above all to transmit to mankind in his Word" (TOB 87:6).

What *does* God wish above all to tell us in his Word? That he loves us, that he has an eternal desire to be *one* with us in the flesh through his Son, Jesus Christ. In a word (or, rather, five), God wants to marry us. John Paul II observes that, while the prophets spoke very boldly of God's spousal love for Israel, this mystery was only "half-open" in the Old Testament. In Ephesians 5, the mystery of God's spousal love is "fully unveiled (without ceasing to be a mystery, of course)" (TOB 95:7). In turn, we become witnesses "of a particular encounter of [God's] mystery with the very essence of the vocation to marriage" (TOB 89:7).

In our prayerful examination of Ephesians 5, we must try "to understand if possible 'to the very depths' what wealth of the truth revealed by God is contained within the scope of [this] stupendous page" (TOB 87:6). This "key and classic text," as John Paul II describes it, not only immerses us in the glory and greatness of God's plan for creating us male and female and calling us to become "one flesh." Even more, it serves as "the compendium or *summa*, in some sense, *of the teaching about God and man* which was brought to fulfillment by Christ."[79]

Here is the entire passage:

> Submit to one another out of reverence for Christ. Wives, submit to your husbands, as to the Lord. For the husband is the head of the wife as Christ is the head of the Church, his body, and is himself its Savior. As the Church submits to Christ, so let wives also submit in everything to their husbands. Husbands, love your wives, as Christ

loved the Church and gave himself up for her, that he might sanctify her, having cleansed her by the washing of water with the word, that he might present the Church to himself in splendor, without spot or wrinkle or any such thing, that she might be holy and without blemish. Even so husbands should love their wives as their own bodies. He who loves his wife loves himself. For no man ever hates his own flesh, but nourishes and cherishes it, as Christ does the Church, because we are members of his body. "For this reason a man shall leave his father and mother and be joined to his wife, and the two shall become one flesh." This is a great mystery, and I mean in reference to Christ and the Church. (Ephesians 5:21–32)

That Controversial Line

If we are to mine the riches of Paul's teaching on the "great mystery" of marriage, we would do well to address head-on the fact that Ephesians 5 contains one of the most controversial lines in the whole Bible: "Wives, submit to your husbands." In Catholic circles today, approaches to this passage usually lean in one of two directions. Many dismiss Paul's teaching out of hand as nothing but a product of the chauvinism of his time, claiming it has nothing whatsoever to say to us in a modern context. Others appeal to Paul's teaching on submission to justify a terribly distorted kind of leadership in marriage that amounts to little more than a veiled form of male domination. By reading the passage in context—both the overall context of Scripture and the cultural context in which Paul was writing—John Paul II offers a very balanced and compelling reading of Paul's teaching on submission that avoids errors on both sides.

Scripture makes it very clear that the tendency of men to dominate women is the specific result of original sin. Before sin, the original order of love called the husband to initiate the gift of self in the image of God. The woman, in turn, recognizing the sincerity of her husband's gift, longed to receive it and return it, thus forming a true "communion of persons." Only *after* original sin and only as *a result of it*, does God say to the woman, "Your desire shall be for your husband, and he shall rule over you" (Genesis 3:16). The verbs translated as "desire" and "rule" both indicate the tragic effects of sin on man and woman's original communion. The initiation of the gift has warped into the sinful tendency to dominate woman, and the woman's longing to receive and return the sincere gift of herself has also warped into a manipulative self-interest.

As we will see, St. Paul is in no way justifying these sinful tendencies in marriage. Quite the contrary: he's calling spouses *back to the original order of love* through the redemption won for them in Christ.

St. Paul's Evangelical Genius

Like all of us, St. Paul was certainly affected by his culture. As John Paul II writes, he "is not afraid to accept the concepts that were characteristic of the mentality and customs of that time . . . Certainly, our contemporary sensitivity is different . . . and the social position of women in comparison with men is different" (TOB 89:5, 6). But if we simply dismiss St. Paul's words as nothing but a product of his "politically incorrect" culture, we miss his evangelical genius altogether. Like any great evangelist, St. Paul appeals to the language and customs of the culture he is trying to reach, while injecting that language and those customs with the mystery of Christ.

In Ephesians 4 (remember, context is key), St. Paul states explicitly that Christians "must no longer live as the Gentiles do." They "are darkened in their understanding . . . due to their hardness of heart." So put off "your old nature which . . . is corrupt through deceitful lusts . . . and be renewed in the spirit of your minds, and put on the new nature, created after the likeness of God in true righteousness and holiness" (Ephesians 4:17–18, 22–24). This should all sound very familiar to us by now. Who also spoke of "hardness of heart" and how it distorts the sexual relationship? Who also invited men and women to live in "true righteousness and holiness" by experiencing redemption from lust? Like Christ, Paul is calling men and women to live according to the divine image in which God originally made them—and he's pointing them to Christ as the Savior who enables them to do so.

When the contested (and detested) verses of Ephesians 5 are read in their full context, we realize that—far from demeaning women and absolving abusive men—St. Paul is restoring the only sure foundation for the proper balance of love between the sexes. In effect, he is saying something like this: "You want to talk about 'submission' in marriage? Fine. But that means one thing to the Gentiles. Here is how it must look for followers of Christ."

Mutual Submission Out of Reverence for Christ

Notice that the first thing St. Paul says to spouses is "Submit to *one another* out of reverence for Christ" (Ephesians 5:21). As John Paul II emphasizes, Ephesians 5 calls spouses to a *mutual* submission. Those who think Saint Paul was simply regurgitating cultural prejudice against women do not understand how countercultural this idea was.

John Paul II insists that St. Paul "does not intend to say that . . . marriage is a contract of domination by the husband over the wife. . . . Love makes the *husband simultaneously subject* to the wife" (TOB 89:3, 4). He adds that being "subject" to one's spouse means being "completely given" (TOB 90:2). Therefore mutual submission means "a reciprocal gift of self" (see TOB 89:4). It means that both spouses realize and live the spousal meaning of their bodies, which calls them to mutual and sincere self-giving.

Christ, who gave up his body for his Bride, must be the source and the model of this self-giving. Christian spouses give themselves up for one another "out of reverence for Christ" (v. 21). John Paul II goes so far as to say that this reverence is nothing other than a *"spiritually mature form"* of the mutual attraction of the sexes, of that *"fascination* of the man for femininity and of the woman for masculinity" (TOB 117b:4). In other words, "reverence for Christ" results from a lived experience of the redemption of sexual attraction and desire, the redemption of eros. Through ongoing conversion we gradually come to experience that mature level of purity we spoke of previously.

Pure men and women *see* the mystery of Christ revealed through their bodies. It's not just a theory or concept; pure men and women *feel* it in their hearts. They realize that the call to union inscribed in their sexuality is a "great mystery" that proclaims the union of Christ and the Church. To the degree that we experience this as the "content" of our sexual attractions, we do not want to lust—we want to *genuflect*. To the degree that we live as St. Paul calls us to, lust becomes distasteful to us. The "great mystery" of sexuality fills us instead with profound amazement, awe, and wonder. In other words, it fills us with *reverence for Christ*.

In turn, this reverence for the "great mystery" revealed through our sexuality opens up realms of freedom and joy previously inaccessible to us. We come to "possess ourselves" and our passions. Eros is no longer in control of us, we are in control of it, and—in delightful freedom—we're able to direct erotic desire toward the sincere gift of self. "The satisfaction of the passions is, in fact, one thing," observes John Paul II, "quite another is the joy a person finds in possessing himself more fully, since in this way he can also become more fully a true gift for another person" (TOB 58:7). Of course, there is always an ever deeper need for purification in this regard. "One can never consider [self-mastery] acquired once and for all. It presupposes renewed effort at all stages of life" (CCC, 2342). But the effort it requires repays us a thousandfold by enabling us to find the "freedom for which Christ has set us free" (Galatians 5:1) and by granting us tastes of the love and joy for which our hearts truly long.

Submission within the Spousal Analogy

If St. Paul is only regurgitating the cultural idea of wives as the "property" of their husbands, the feminist revolt against Ephesians 5 is quite understandable. In the absence of redemption, Paul's words can only be viewed as an admonition for wives to resign themselves to male lust and tyranny. But redemption has been accomplished! The knowledge that Christ died and rose again to empower us to live according to God's original plan of love deeply imbues the apostle's entire teaching on marriage. In fact, he presents redemption itself through the analogy of spousal love and sexual union.

According to the analogy, the wife images the Church and the husband images Christ. The analogy obviously breaks down (e.g., no husband perfectly images Christ, nor does any wife perfectly image the "spotless bride" of Christ), yet it speaks volumes not only about Christ's spousal love for us, but also about the very essence and meaning of marriage. We learn that "marriage corresponds to the vocation of Christians only when it mirrors the love that Christ, the Bridegroom, gives to the Church, his bride, and which the Church . . . seeks to give back to Christ" (TOB 90:2). Apart from this model, marriage can sink quite quickly into a form of oppression, especially for women.

Again, St. Paul uses the language of his day but injects it with an entirely new, redemptive meaning. When we understand the nature of the analogy he is using, it makes sense for him to say, "Wives, submit to your husbands, *as to the Lord*" (v. 22). One way I explain submission in this context is, "Wives, put yourself under (sub) the mission of your husband." What's the mission of the husband? "Husbands, love your wives as Christ loved the Church." How did Christ love the Church? He "gave himself up for her" (v. 25)—unto death! Christ said that he came not to *be* served but *to serve*, to lay down his life for his Bride (see Matthew 20:28).

"Headship" Is a Call to Serve

Perhaps our quickness to accuse Paul of justifying male domination says more about our hang-ups today than his back then. Based on what we've unfolded, when Paul writes, "Wives, submit to your husbands" he is saying, "Wives, allow your husbands to *serve you . . . unto death*." Wow. Our typical interpretation of Paul's words is flipped upside down! Not that the wife is the master and the husband a slave—power, control, domination . . . these are the wrong paradigms altogether.

Christian marriage calls husband and wife to a *mutual service*. Yet, according to the nature of sexual difference, each lives this service in different, complementary ways.

If Ephesians says that "the husband is the head of the wife as Christ is the head of the Church," this means the husband must be *the first to serve* (see Luke 22:25–26). There is a "sacred order" to love. In imaging Christ and the Church, John Paul II writes that "the husband is above all *he who loves*, and the wife, on the other hand is *she who is loved*." Thus, we can conclude that "the wife's 'submission' to the husband . . . means above all 'the experiencing of love.' This is all the more so, because this 'submission' refers to the image of the submission of the Church to Christ, which certainly consists in experiencing his love" (TOB 92:6).

We can and should apply this attitude of being "first to serve" in all areas of married life. But what might it look like in the marriage bed? John Paul II wrote that if a husband is truly to love his wife, "it is necessary to insist that intercourse must not serve merely as a means of allowing [his] climax. . . . The man must take [the] difference between male and female reactions into account . . . so that climax may be reached [by] both . . . and as far as possible occur in both simultaneously." The husband must do this "not for hedonistic, but for altruistic reasons." In this case, if "we take into account the shorter . . . curve of arousal in the man, [such] tenderness on his part in the context of marital intercourse acquires the significance of an act of virtue."[80] (Please read this passage to anyone who thinks the Church is "down on sex." How far from the truth! As an astonished engaged woman once exclaimed when I read this passage at her marriage-prep class, "The pope rocks!")

Mutual climax is not always possible for a host of understandable reasons, but we all know the stereotypical image of the selfish husband who takes his pleasure, then rolls over and falls asleep. Such a man cannot be said to love his wife "as Christ loves the Church." Christ wants his Bride to receive and remain in the fullness of his love so that his joy may be in her and her joy may be complete (see John 15:9–11). And, yes, marital intercourse is meant to be an expression and experience of this joy!

The Journey Toward Healing

History attests that few men have allowed St. Paul's words to challenge their selfish inclinations to lust and domination. Instead, we've often used his words to justify our sinful attitudes and behavior. Of course, it's a two-way street. History also demonstrates that women know how to use and manipulate men just as much as men know how to use and manipulate women. That said, women have suffered in a particular way throughout history at the hands of male lust and domination, and, as we mentioned earlier, men seem to have a special responsibility to restore the proper balance of love between the sexes (see TOB 33:2).

How do we begin the long journey toward healing? Christ calls us first and foremost to repentance. In that light, I would like to ask all the women reading this book to allow me, as a representative of the male side of the human race, to apologize humbly for the way male lust and domination have wounded you. The wounds go so very deep in a woman's soul, and I am very, very sorry.

For the ways we have treated you in thought or deed as an object for our own pleasure and enjoyment, please forgive us.

For the ways we have ignored you or rejected you because you haven't met our impossible standards of "beauty" or haven't aroused our lusts, please forgive us.

For the ways we have seen your differences as a threat to our own fragile sense of security rather than a complement and a gift, please forgive us.

For the ways we have used our strength to manipulate and control you rather than honor and serve you, please forgive us.

For the pride and sense of superiority that have led us to ignore your counsel and belittle your point of view, please forgive us.

In all the ways we have failed to love you as Christ loves the Church, please forgive us. We know not what we do. *Jesus, please lead us to the fullness of healing.*

Restoration of Holiness

Recall that every married couple has "run out of wine." Spouses who commit themselves to St. Paul's vision of marriage—properly understood—find that, through all the trials and difficulties of married life, God's grace restores the wine in superabundance. Uniting all of their sorrows and sufferings with those of Christ in his crucifixion, spouses also come to experience the joy of Christ's Resurrection. In this way, spouses experience their love for each other as something beautifully healing and redemptive.

There is only one Creator. And yet, as we learn in the first pages of Genesis, God shares his creative power with spouses, enabling them to bring new human life into the world. Similarly, there is only one Redeemer. And yet, as we learn in Ephesians

5, God shares his redeeming power with spouses, enabling them to bring new life in Christ to each other. As John Paul II says, when spouses love each other with the love of Christ, marital love becomes "redeeming, saving love, the love with which man has been loved by God from eternity in Christ" (TOB 90:2). Here we see very clearly the divine dimension of the sacrament, the divine gift and grace communicated through marriage.

Even here on earth, the grace of Christ's spousal love begins restoring in us something of the holiness experienced by the first married couple. "Christ loved the Church and gave himself up for her . . . that she might be holy" (vv. 25–27). But, as we all know, holiness is not something automatic. In all our trials and struggles, we must continually open ourselves like a bride to receive the gift of Christ's love, allowing it to *in*form and *trans*form us. As John Paul II writes, "Holiness is measured according to the 'great mystery' in which the Bride responds with the gift of love to the gift of the Bridegroom."[81] Here the Bride refers to all of us (male and female) in relation to Christ the Bridegroom.

Holiness, then, is not first a matter of *doing*, but of *letting it be done to us* (see Luke 1:38). We must allow Christ to put to death all our disordered ways of relating. We must allow him to sanctify us, to make us holy, "by the washing of water with the word" (v. 26). Scripture scholars see in this a reference to baptism. It was customary in St. Paul's day for the bride to precede her wedding with a cleansing bath in preparation for her bridegroom. The *Catechism* describes baptism as "the nuptial bath which precedes the wedding feast, the Eucharist" (*CCC*, 1617). St. Paul also alludes to the nuptial gift of the Eucharist when he speaks of the "nourishment" Christ offers his Bride (see v. 29).

But marriage not only sheds light on baptism and the Eucharist. John Paul II observes that marriage serves as the model or *prototype* in some sense of all the sacraments of the new covenant (see TOB 98:2). All the sacraments have a spousal character since their purpose is to unite the Bride (the Church) with her Bridegroom (Christ) and allow the Bride to conceive eternal life. Through this grand analogy, the union of spouses becomes perhaps the most insightful way of understanding Christianity itself. "The entire Christian life bears the mark of the spousal love of Christ and the Church" (CCC, 1617).

Chosen in Christ from the Beginning

Just as God organically inscribed the union of Adam and Eve in the mystery of creation, he organically inscribes the union of the new Adam and the new Eve (Christ and the Church) in the mystery of redemption. Spousal union, in fact, becomes the foundation upon which God constructs the entire mystery of our redemption in Christ (see TOB 95b:7). The mystery of redemption "clothes itself, so to speak, in the figure and form of the primordial sacrament [of marriage]. To the marriage of the first husband and wife . . . corresponds the marriage, or rather the analogy of marriage, of Christ with the Church" (TOB 97:2).

Here, in the spousal character of both creation and redemption, we recognize an essential continuity regarding God's plan for humanity. We tend to think of Christ's coming as "Plan B," necessitated when man and woman's sin supposedly thwarted "Plan A." Our need of redemption from sin certainly flows from the reality of our fall. Yet God's plan for us to share in his own eternal exchange of love remains the same yesterday, today, and forever. Sin, you might say, caused a detour in the fulfillment of that plan, but it didn't thwart it. God's plan for man continues despite sin. "The plan of the Lord stands forever" (Psalm 33:11). That plan—forever and for always—is that all things would be taken up and united in Christ (see Ephesians 1:10).

John Paul II cannot stress enough that Christ—the incarnate Christ—has always been at the center of God's plan for man and for the universe. As he wrote in the first line of his first encyclical letter, "Jesus Christ is the center of the universe and of history."[82] God destined us for union with Christ not only after sin and not only to redeem us from sin. God "chose us in [Christ] before the foundation of the world" (Ephesians 1:4). *This* is the divine gift that marriage communicates to the world; *this* is the story our bodies tell: we've been chosen in Christ to be united with God forever in an eternal covenant of love!

This means that the grace of original innocence (recall the experiences of original solitude, unity, and nakedness) "was granted in consideration of him [Christ] . . . although— according to the dimensions of time and history—it preceded the Incarnation" (TOB 96:5). In other words, the love and grace man and woman knew "in the beginning" through their bodies was a foretaste or preview in some sense of the love and grace that Christ would pour out within history through his body. In fact, the love the first couple knew in their bodies *depended* in some sense on the love that Christ would pour out on his Bride, the Church. Creation foreshadows and prepares us for redemption; the union of the first Adam and Eve foreshadows and prepares us for the union of the new Adam and Eve, Christ and the Church.

Again, although it often demands a rethinking of commonly held perceptions, the Incarnation is not an afterthought in God's mind. As the *Catechism* confirms, "From the beginning, God envisaged the glory of the new creation in Christ" (*CCC*, 280). We can conclude this because St. Paul links the one-flesh union of Genesis with the union of Christ and the Church. "'For this reason a man shall leave his father and mother and be joined to his wife, and the two shall become one flesh.' This is a great mystery, and I mean in reference to Christ and the Church" (Ephesians 5:31–32). "By becoming one flesh, [husband and wife] embody the espousal of our human nature by the Son of God."[83] And this means that right from the beginning—before sin—conjugal union foreshadowed the Incarnation, Christ's union with humanity in one flesh.

This Is a "Great Mystery"

St. Paul's linking of the one-flesh union with the union of Christ and the Church "is the most important point of the whole text, *in some sense its keystone*" (TOB 93:1). Both "the union of Christ with the Church and the spousal union of man and woman in marriage are in this way illuminated by a particular supernatural light" (TOB 91:8).

Guided by this supernatural light, St. Paul demonstrates a keen understanding of the sacramentality of the body. Recall the broader sense of this term. The body is a "sacrament" in the sense that it makes visible the invisible. In examining Ephesians 5, John Paul II recalls his thesis: "The body, in fact, and only the body, is capable of making visible what is invisible: the spiritual and divine. It has been created to transfer into the visible reality of the world the mystery hidden from eternity in God, and thus to be a sign of it" (TOB 96:6, 19:4).

Recall what we mean by "the mystery hidden from eternity in God": 1) *God is a Communion of love,* and 2) we are *destined to share in that exchange* through our union with Christ. Our beloved Polish saint writes that the "sacrament consists in *'manifesting'* that *mystery in a sign* that serves not only to proclaim the mystery but also *to accomplish it* in man" (TOB 93:5). Sacramental signs truly bring about what they signify. The author of Ephesians speaks of two signs—one from the order of creation and the other from the order of redemption—that truly communicate God's mystery of love.

In creation, John Paul II says that God's mystery of love "became a *visible reality through the union* of the first man and woman" (see Genesis 2:24). In redemption, that same mystery of love becomes "*a visible reality in the indissoluble union of Christ with the Church,* which the author of Ephesians presents as the spousal union" (TOB 97:4). With regard to these signs, these two unions, we are speaking "in reference to the entire work of creation and redemption" (TOB 97:5). This is the stupendous capacity of sacramental signs. They mysteriously "contain" ultimate reality and put us in touch with it. They "embrace the universe," as John Paul II says.

The Meaning of Human Life

John Paul II remarks that it is a "particular merit" of the apostle Paul "that he brought these two signs together [the one-flesh union and the union of Christ and the Church], making of them *the single great sign,* that is, *a great sacrament* (TOB 95b:7). Through this great sacrament the "great mystery" of human life is revealed.

The linking of these two unions is obviously important "to the Christian vocation of husbands and wives." However, it "is equally essential and valid *for the [understanding] of man* in general: for the fundamental problem of understanding him and for the self-understanding of his being in the world." Indeed, it is in this link that we "find the answer to the question about the meaning of 'being a body'" (TOB 102:5).

What is that meaning? We are called to love as Christ loves. This is the new commandment Christ gives us, "Love one another as I have loved you" (John 15:12). How did Christ love us? "This is my body . . . *given for you*" (Luke 22:19). Here, in the Eucharist, Christ not only shows us the meaning of love. His body received also empowers us to love others in the same way, and to recognize that this is the story our bodies tell.

Remember the tears of my father-in-law when he received the Eucharist for the first time after consummating his marriage? He realized that day that the meaning of life, the meaning of the universe, is inscribed not only in our souls, but in our bodies: in the "great mystery" of sexual difference and our call to become one flesh. As we will see even more clearly in the next chapter, spousal union is the "great sign" God has given the world to reveal the "great mystery" of his own life and love. And *that* is what that young couple's passion has to do with "the stars."

FOR REFLECTION

1. If the number one ingredient for a successful marriage is mercy, how do you see this quality reflected in your own marriage (or, if you are single, in the marriages of those close to you)?

2. How do you think the calling of husband and wife in marriage is similar? How is it different? How are these differences revealed in the body?

3. St. Paul's use of the word "submission" is terribly misunderstood in today's society. Based on what you've learned in the TOB, how would you explain this to someone who thinks being submissive is the equivalent of being a doormat?

Come, Holy Spirit. Give us the eyes to see the "great mystery" of Christ's love for the Church revealed through our bodies as male and female. Give us the grace to confront the lies we have believed that make it so difficult for us to love, accept, and understand our bodies as God the Father created them to be. Dislodge these lies from our hearts, that we might live in the full freedom Christ won for us through his body given up for us. Amen.

SEVEN

Marriage as a Human Sign of Divine Love

Authentic married love is caught up into divine love.
—*The Second Vatican Council*

As you may have guessed, I never wrote that book—*Loving Her Rightly*. If I ever do, I imagine it will be coauthored by Wendy West.

Perhaps chief among the lessons my marriage continues to teach me is that I don't need to hide my faults, sins, and weaknesses in order to be lovable. Somehow I had absorbed a very different message growing up, and it created a rather crippling perfectionism in my life from which I'm still recovering long into adulthood.

It seems many people think a saint is someone who has it all together, and so that's what we strive for. But the only way to accomplish that is by burying all of our brokenness and pretending it isn't there. Pope Benedict XVI set the record straight when he insisted that "the saints have not 'fallen from Heaven.' They are people like us, who also have complicated problems." What a relief! He continues:

Holiness does not consist in never having erred or sinned. Holiness increases the capacity for conversion, for repentance, for willingness to start again and, especially, for reconciliation and forgiveness. . . . Consequently, it is not the fact that we have never erred but our capacity for reconciliation and forgiveness which makes us saints. And we can all learn this way of holiness.[84]

Rather than burying our brokenness, we must confess it. "Confession" is not just the name of one of the seven sacraments, it's a bedrock principle of the Christian life that's meant to reverse the effect of the fall in our hearts. Since the dawn of original sin, we've been hiding our "nakedness" from God (and one another) out of fear that we're not lovable. Faith in God's love casts this fear out (see 1 John 4:18), enabling us to bring all of our brokenness into the light, knowing we will not be chided or condemned, but embraced, forgiven, healed. "I was afraid, because I was naked; so I hid myself" is transformed into "I was at peace, because I know God loves me in my nakedness; so I exposed myself."

This is the kind of love spouses are meant to share with one another: the love that allows them to be "naked without shame"— to "see and know each other . . . with all the peace of the interior gaze" (TOB 13:1). As we know well, it's at the deepest spiritual level of our humanity—not merely the physical level—that we're afraid of our "nakedness" and, thus, find ourselves "hiding." True love, however, is not afraid of the other person's "warts." In fact, the "strength of such a love emerges most clearly," John Paul II tells us, "when the beloved person stumbles, when his or her weaknesses or even sins come into the open. One who truly loves does not then withdraw his love, but loves all the more, loves in full consciousness of the other's shortcomings and faults. . . . For the person as such never loses its essential value."[85]

Becoming a Human Sign of Divine Love

As we will learn more clearly in this chapter, the indispensable path to learning how to love in this healing, redemptive way is learning how to pray in this healing, redemptive way. True, intimate prayer, the *Catechism* tells us, is where we "let our masks fall" so as to let the Lord love us as we really are, handing "ourselves over to him as an offering to be purified and transformed." In turn, as we learn to "welcome the love by which we are loved," the forgiven sinner wants to respond by loving others in the same way (see *CCC*, 2711–12).

In other words, by receiving the *divine love* by which we are loved, we can become *human signs* of that love to others. And *that* is what the sacrament of marriage is all about. In the last chapter, we looked primarily at the *divine dimension* of the sacrament. Now we will look more closely at the *human dimension* of the sacrament—the physical, bodily sign through which God communicates his love through husband and wife.

We have already said much about the nature of marital love as a sign of God's love. But now John Paul II gets even more specific. He does so first by developing the concept of the "language of the body" and the need to speak this language truthfully. Then he looks to the lovers in the Song of Songs and to the marriage of Tobias and Sarah as biblical examples of couples who, each in their own way, speak the language of the body truthfully. As John Paul II says, both couples "find their place in what constitutes the sacramental sign of marriage. Both share in the [truthful] formation of this sign" (TOB 116:5).

The Sacramental Sign of Marriage

Every sacrament has a specific physical sign that communicates the spiritual reality it signifies. For example, the physical sign of baptism—the bathing of a person with water—really and truly communicates a spiritual cleansing of the person's soul from original sin. What, then, is the physical sign of the sacrament of marriage that communicates the spiritual mystery of God's love to the couple and, through them, to their children and the whole world?

Over the centuries there have basically been two schools of thought. Some theologians have considered the exchange of vows (marital consent) to be the sign of marriage. Others have taught that the consummation of marriage in sexual intercourse is that sign. In effect, by demonstrating the integral relationship between the marriage vows and the act of intercourse, John Paul II says *both* views are correct, so long as they are properly held together (see TOB 103:3).

He observes that the sacramental sign of marriage is one of "manifold contents" (see TOB 105:6). It begins with the exchange of consent, is consummated in sexual intercourse, and is borne in the spouses themselves throughout the whole of their married lives. What makes the husband and wife themselves a sacramental sign of God's spiritual and divine love? *Their bodies* as male and female—and the "one body" they become. As a sacrament, marriage is "a *sign that* efficaciously [really, truly, effectively] *transmits in the visible world the invisible mystery hidden in God from eternity.* And this is the mystery of Truth and Love, the mystery of divine life, in which man really participates." This sign "is constituted with man, inasmuch as he is a 'body,' through his 'visible' masculinity and femininity" (TOB 19:4).

Wedding vows are an outward sign in as much as they express something spiritual—the commitment of the heart to love as God loves. But if this spiritual commitment is to be made flesh, the "language of the heart" must have a corresponding "language of the body."

The Language of the Body

We all know that the body speaks a language. We can say a great deal without uttering a word through bodily gestures. A wave of the hand says "hello" or "good bye." A shrug of the shoulders says, "I don't know." A raised fist expresses anger.

The body also speaks an amazingly profound language in sexual intercourse. As John Paul II candidly expresses, "Through gestures and reactions, through the whole . . . dynamism of tension and enjoyment—whose direct source is the body in its masculinity and femininity, the body in its action and interaction—through all this *man, the person,* 'speaks' . . . Precisely on the level of this 'language of the body' . . . man and woman reciprocally express *themselves* in the fullest and most profound way made possible for them by . . . their masculinity and femininity" (TOB 123:4).

But what is sexual intercourse meant to express? What is its true language, its true meaning? As we've been learning throughout our exploration of John Paul II's TOB, the bodily union of a man and a woman is designed by the Creator to express and communicate the "great mystery" of divine love, of Christ's union with the Church (see Ephesians 5:31–32). Whether we realize it or not, this is the astounding power of the language of our bodies: "bodily love" is meant to express "the language of 'agape'" (TOB 92:7). However, in order to speak this language, we must properly understand it.

Incarnating Divine Love

"Love one another as I have loved you" (John 15:12). This "new commandment" of Jesus summarizes the very meaning of life. It's a commandment that God inscribed right from the beginning not in stone tablets, but in the very mystery of our bodies, in the very mysteries of sex, gender, and marriage. It's a commandment he inscribed in the spousal meaning of our bodies as male and female.

How did Christ love us? "This is my body . . . given for you. . . . This cup is the new covenant in my blood, which is poured out for you" (Luke 22:19–20). These are the Lord's wedding vows, offered to his Bride at the Last Supper as a verbal expression of the language of his heart. Then, when he lay down on "the marriage bed of the cross," he expressed the same covenant love without words, through the language of his body. In this way, Christ superabundantly fulfilled the spousal meaning of the body by showing us "to the end" what spousal love *is*, what it calls us to, what it demands of us, and, through his resurrection, what it rewards those who—notwithstanding their own limitations, weaknesses, and sins—entrust themselves to God's grace and mercy and embrace the truth of spousal love with all their hearts.

Without that entrustment to God's grace and mercy, those same limitations, weaknesses, and sins incline us very powerfully toward a "love" that is riddled with selfishness and egoism. Thus, we must constantly challenge ourselves to distinguish true love from its many distortions and falsifications by measuring everything we call "love" against Christ's love.

How does Christ love? First, he gives himself *freely*: "No one takes my life from me, I lay it down of my own accord" (John 10:18). Second, he gives himself *totally*: without reservation, condition, or selfish calculation: "He loved them to the last" (John 13:1). Third, he gives himself *faithfully*: "I am with you always" (Matthew 28:20). And fourth, he gives himself *fruitfully*: "I came that they may have life" (John 10:10). If men and women are to speak the true language of their bodies, they must learn continually and ever more deeply to open themselves to Christ's love, letting it bear fruit in them, so that they can, in turn, share this same *free, total, faithful, fruitful* love with each other.

Committing to love in this way has a name: it's called *marriage*. This, in fact, is precisely what a bride and groom commit to at the altar. The priest or deacon asks them: "Have you come here *freely* and *without reservation* to give yourselves to each other in marriage? Do you promise to be *faithful* all the days of your lives? Do you promise to *receive children* lovingly from God?" When the bride and groom each say "yes," that word expresses the language of their hearts: This is what we want; this is what we desire— to love as Christ loves. In turn, spouses are meant to express that same "yes" of their hearts with the language of their bodies whenever they become one flesh. "In fact, the words themselves, 'I take you as my wife/as my husband,'" John Paul II says, "can only be fulfilled by conjugal intercourse" (TOB 103:2). With conjugal intercourse "we pass *to the reality* that corresponds to these words.

Both the one and the other element are important *with regard to the structure of the sacramental sign*" (TOB 103:3). "Sexual union, lovingly experienced and sanctified by the sacrament, is in turn a path of growth in the life of grace for the couple," affirms Pope Francis. "It is the 'nuptial mystery' [revealing Christ's love for the Church]."[86]

Sexual intercourse is where the words of the wedding vows *become flesh*. It's where husband and wife are meant to *incarnate* divine love. It's a fine thing when a couple return to the Church to renew their vows on a special anniversary, but this shouldn't undermine the fact that every time a husband and wife have intercourse they are meant to renew their wedding vows with the language of their bodies. The Church's sexual ethic begins to make beautiful and compelling sense when viewed through this lens. The Church's teaching is not a prudish list of prohibitions. It's a call to embrace our own greatness, our own God-given dignity. It's a call to live the love we're created for, the love we so ardently desire.

Distinguishing True and False Prophets

John Paul II goes so far as to describe the language of the body in sexual union as something "prophetic." A prophet is someone who speaks for God, who proclaims his mystery. This is what the marital embrace is meant to proclaim. But, as he adds, we must be careful to distinguish true and false prophets (see TOB 106:4). If we can speak the truth with our bodies, we can also speak lies.

We all know it is possible to lie with our bodies. Suppose a used-car salesman knowingly sells you a lemon and then shakes your hand. Didn't he just lie with his body? What about the kiss of Judas? It was a lie. And who do you think prompts us to lie with our bodies? The "father of lies" is hell-bent on getting us to speak his own language with our bodies. Why? To keep us from the "great mystery" of Christ's union with the Church—that is, to keep us from eternal life.

Recall from chapter one that the battle for man's soul is fought over the truth of his body. If the body is meant to sing the greatest of all songs—the Song of Songs—we must be well aware that there is an enemy who hates the divine-human harmony of this song and eagerly wants to insert his own sour notes. If God designed the body to be a sign of his own love and life, the enemy wants to counter that sign with lust and death. As John Paul II observed, when spouses "unite as husband and wife, they . . . find themselves in the situation in which *the powers of good and evil fight against each other.*" Their choices and acts, in fact, "take on the whole weight of human existence in the union of the two" (TOB 115:2, 3).

How, then, in the midst of such a sobering battle, can men and women be sure that love and life will win? John Paul II turns to the lovers of the Song of Songs and the marriage of Tobias and Sarah as two shining examples of married couples who "read the language of the body in truth" and thus experience the triumph of love and life over lust and death.

The Agony and the Ecstasy

John Paul II's insights into the Song of Songs and the marriage of Tobias and Sarah are incredibly rich. They also take us into themes so intimate that he deemed it necessary to deliver an abridged version in the public audiences of the TOB. The unabridged version of this section of the TOB was not made available in the English-speaking world until 2006. Soon thereafter, I devoted an entire book to these "hidden talks" of the TOB, called *Heaven's Song: Sexual Love as It Was Meant to Be*. In what follows, I only scratch the surface of what I cover there.

In short, if the Song of Songs reveals the *ecstasy* of becoming one flesh, the marriage of Tobias and Sarah reveals the *agony*. Only by holding the two together do we get a realistic vision of the sacrament of marriage. It can seem as if those who promote Catholic teaching are afraid it won't go over so well if we talk about the real sufferings involved in following Jesus. So, at times, we can promote the glories of the Christian life without a realistic assessment of the sorrows. I, too, have probably been guilty of that on occasion.

In light of how many people believe the Church is "down on sex," the glories and ecstasies to which authentic Catholic teaching calls spouses (as exemplified in the Song of Songs) *should* be emphasized. But these glories and ecstasies are the fruit of embracing *much* purifying suffering (as exemplified in the marriage of Tobias and Sarah). If the joy is not set before us, we will have no motivation to endure the suffering: "For the joy set before him Christ endured the cross" (Hebrews 12:2). But if the path to those joys is not also realistically assessed, we will naively wonder why marriage can be so difficult, even agonizing. Let us strive for the ecstasy of the couple in the Song of Songs! But let us not be surprised that that joy comes only through the "battle" endured by Tobias and Sarah.

The Biblical Ode to Erotic Love

Why is the Song of Songs the favorite biblical book of so many of the greatest saints and mystics? Why have they written more commentaries on the Song of Songs than on any other book in the Bible? St. Gregory of Nyssa provides the answer when he observes that human nature "can neither discover nor entertain anything greater" than "the mystery contained in the Song of Songs." The superlative nature of the title itself tells us that Christ "promises to teach us mysteries of mysteries by the agency of the Song of Songs."[87]

And that "agency," St. Gregory reminds us, is "the passion of erotic love." This "most intense of pleasurable activities . . . is set as a figure at the very fore of the guidance that the teachings give so that we may learn that it is necessary for the soul [to] . . . boil with love . . . heated by that 'fire' which the Lord came to 'cast upon the earth' (Luke 12:49)."[88]

God's eternal plan, let us remember, is to marry us—to live with us in an eternal union of love that the Bible compares to the union of spouses in one flesh. Recall Pope Benedict XVI's statement that the Song of Songs expresses "the essence of biblical faith."[89] And the essence of that faith is this: We can enter into "nuptial union" with God, our primordial aspiration. The erotic love poetry of the Song of Songs gives us entrance to the wedding feast that never ends. It transposes heaven's love song into an earthly key, enabling us to "hit the notes," so to speak.

Yet the Song of Songs is not merely an allegory of God's "spiritual" love. John Paul II observes that a growing number of biblical scholars maintain that the Song of Songs is "to be taken simply as what it manifestly is: a song of human love" (TOB 108, note 95). For "human love, created and blessed by God, can be the theme of an inspired biblical book" (TOB 108, note 97).

John Paul II seems to agree with the view of one scholar who writes that those who have "forgotten the lovers" or "petrified them into pretense" have not interpreted the Song correctly.

"'He who does not believe in the human love of the spouses, he who must ask forgiveness for the body, does not have the right to rise higher. ... . With the affirmation of human love, by contrast, it is possible to discover the revelation of God in it'" (TOB 108, note 96). Indeed, it's precisely in the experience of authentic human love that we encounter divine love. "Hence," as Pope Francis affirms, "those who have deep spiritual aspirations should not feel that [being married and raising a family] detracts from their growth in the life of the Spirit, but rather see it as a path which the Lord is using to lead them to the heights of mystical union."[90]

This confirms an essential element of incarnational/sacramental reality. Grace—the mystery of God's life and covenant love—is communicated *through* the "stuff" of our humanity, not despite it. The content of the Song of Songs is at the same time sexual and sacred. When we ignore the sacred, we see the Song merely as a secular erotic poem. But when we ignore the sexual in favor of a disembodied allegory of God's love, we fall into *allegorism*. "It is only by putting [the sexual and the sacred] together that one can read the book in the right way" (TOB 108, note 97).

Recall that our goal in this chapter is to reflect on the human dimension of marriage as a physical sign of God's life and love. This is precisely what the erotic poetry of the Song of Songs helps us to do.

The Bride as "Sister"

Interestingly, the lover in the Song repeatedly refers to his beloved as "sister" *before* calling her "bride." "You have ravished my heart, my sister, my bride, you have ravished my heart with one glance of your eyes . . . How sweet is your love, my sister, my bride!" (4:9–10). These words are "impregnated," John Paul II says, "with a particular content" (TOB 110:1). It is as if the lovers in the Song had "descended from the same family circle, as though from infancy they had been united by memories of the common hearth. In this way, they reciprocally feel as close as brother and sister who owe their existence to the same mother" (TOB 110:1).

Through marriage "man and woman become brother and sister in a special way" (TOB 114:3). Authentic marital love always recognizes one's spouse as a brother or sister who shares the same humanity. It always recognizes that both male and female are made in the image and likeness of God. In this way, calling his beloved "sister" echoes Adam's words, "This at last is bone of my bones and flesh of my flesh" (Genesis 2:23).

Although the idea of being recognized first as a "sister" usually brings a certain relief to the woman, John Paul II observes that it presents a particular *challenge* for the man (see TOB 109:4). Specifically, it challenges him to assess his motives. Is he motivated by love or by lust, by the sincere gift of self or merely by a desire to gratify himself? The normal man recoils at the idea of lusting after his sister—*and so should a man recoil at the thought of lusting after his bride!* This is precisely the point. The lover of the Song accepts this challenge and does not hesitate to call his beloved "sister." With such a recognition, he demonstrates that his desire for her as "bride" is not one of lust but of love. With *"a disinterested tenderness"* (TOB 110:2), the lover desires only to be a sincere gift to his beloved according to the image of God. No man will ever live this perfectly, but our very weakness in this regard can become a channel of God's strength when opened up to his healing love.

Garden Closed, Fountain Sealed

The groom of the Song demonstrates the genuine character of his love all the more when he says, "A garden locked is my sister, my bride, a garden closed, a fountain sealed" (4:12). John Paul II observes that these metaphors remain in a very strict relation with the one-flesh union and, thus, help us to understand its mystery, especially that aspect of the mystery revealed through the woman (see TOB 110:7). We can see the great value of these expressions, he says, in their ability to convey the profoundly personal dimension and meaning of the sexual embrace. "The language of metaphors—poetic language—seems to be especially appropriate and precise in this sphere" (TOB 110:8).

Both these metaphors—"garden closed" and "fountain sealed"—express the whole *personal dignity of the female sex*. They speak with profound reverence of the mystery of the feminine body and, since the body expresses the person, of the feminine personality. These expressions indicate, as John Paul II poignantly observes, that the "bride *presents herself to the eyes of the man as the master of her own mystery*" (TOB 110:7). The groom must—and in the Song of Songs does—respect the fact that he cannot "master" his bride: he cannot, must not, dominate or control her. She is in control of her own person, her own "mystery." For every human person is an inviolable mystery as a unique reflection of God's own mystery.

The point is that authentic love affords a certain entering into the mystery of the other person *without ever violating the mystery of the person* (see TOB 111:1). If a person's "love" violates the one loved, then *it is not love* and should not be called love. It is love's counterfeit—lust. If the lover is to enter this "garden" and participate in the woman's mystery, he cannot barge in or break down the door. Nor can he manipulate her into surrendering the key. This could only violate her. If he is to respect woman as master of her own mystery, all the lover can do is entrust himself to her freedom. All he can do is "knock at the garden gate" and respectfully await her response.

The lover in the Song initiates the gift, making his desire clear: "Open to me, my sister, my love, my dove, my perfect one; for my head is wet with dew." And she hears him: "Listen, my beloved is knocking" (5:2). But he puts "his hand to the latch" (5:4) only with her freely given "yes"—a yes given without any hint of being coerced or manipulated. In total freedom, she surrenders to him; she opens her garden to him, making it *his*: "Awake, O north wind, and come, O south wind! Blow upon my garden, let its fragrance be wafted abroad. Let my beloved come to his garden, and eat its choicest fruits" (4:16).

Thus, in the course of their dialogue of love, *"the 'garden closed' opens up in some way before the eyes of the bridegroom's soul and body"* (TOB 111:4). And with profound reverence and awe ("Submit to one another *out of reverence . . .*") he beholds her mystery unveiled. He comes to her delighting in her gift, remaining ever in awe of her freely opened garden: "I come to my garden, my sister, my bride, I gather my myrrh with my spice, I eat my honeycomb with my honey, I drink my wine with my milk" (5:1).

These boldly erotic verses of this Song of Songs reveal the mystery of "authentic love" (TOB 110:9) and provide an "essential sign of holiness" (TOB 109:2). In other words, by correctly "reading" the language of their bodies, the spouses are not only *speaking* the truth of divine love, they're *singing* it. Their love is in tune with God's love song. That's what makes their love the Song of all Songs. In this way, the human dimension of their sacrament (their human love and sexual union) truly communicates the divine dimension (God's love and grace).

Set Me as a Seal

Sexual intercourse, as the act of marital consummation, is the specific moment in which the marriage bond becomes absolutely indissoluble by anything but death. In this way, "the man and the woman together . . . constitute the sign of the reciprocal gift of self, which *sets the seal on their whole life*" (TOB 111:5). This is the *power* and *meaning* of sexual union as God designed it. Sexual intercourse has a language that proclaims: "I am totally yours unto death. I belong to you and you to me until death do us part."

It's not just that sexual union belongs "in" marriage. Rather, it is that sexual union—as God designed it—has an inherently *marital* meaning. That's why spouses alone can honestly engage in what is properly called the *marital* embrace. To view Church teaching in this regard merely as a "restriction" is to fail altogether to see the grandeur and the glory of what sex *means*. As we learn in the Song of Songs, sex is only what it is meant to be when it expresses a love that is "strong as death" (8:6) and, as such, overcomes the grave in union with Christ. This is what makes authentic sexual love "a promise of immortality" (*CCC*, 2347). Can we imagine any greater evaluation of sexuality than that?

The bride in the Song confirms her knowledge of the greatness of sexual love when she says, "Set me as a seal upon your heart . . . for love is strong as death, . . . Its flashes are flashes of fire, a most vehement flame. Many waters cannot quench love, neither can floods drown it" (8:6–7). John Paul II observes that these words bring us to "the peak" of the Song's declaration of love. They seem to present the final chords of the Song, the "final chords in the 'language of the body.'" When we read that "love is strong as death" we discover "the closure and crowning of everything in the Song of Songs that begins with the metaphor 'garden closed' and 'fountain sealed'" (TOB 111:6).

With these words, the lover presented himself to his beloved not as one superficially attracted to her body. Rather, he presented himself as one who was captivated and fascinated by her entire mystery as a woman, as one ready to uphold the whole personal dignity of her sexuality, as one desirous of honoring her as a feminine person, as a sister and a bride—unto death and for the sake of ensuring a glorious eternity. Here we see that a woman can open her sacred "garden" to her lover and remain inviolate only if she is assured that he is ready and willing to commit his *entire life* to her, if she is assured that he has set her *as a seal upon his heart*, if she is assured that his love will be *strong as death*. This love is called "marriage."

The Church does not impose on us the idea that love should be permanent. Permanence is what the heart longs for. Turn on the radio and you will hear song after song proclaiming this desire for a love that lasts forever. In her teaching that sex is meant to express lasting love (that is, marital love), the Church is simply inviting us to be true to the "song" that wells up from the deepest recesses of our souls. Listen to it! It's the Song of Songs.

Sexual Union Is a Test of Life or Death

If the lovers in the Song of Songs help us distinguish between authentic love and lust, the marriage of Tobias and Sarah in the

Book of Tobit demonstrates just what is at stake in this distinction. From the first moment of their marriage, Tobias and Sarah had *to face the test of life or death*. "The words about love 'strong as death,' spoken by the spouses of the Song of Songs . . . here take on the character of a real test" (TOB 114:6). If we want to live and embrace eros as a "promise of immortality" (*CCC*, 2347), like Tobias and Sarah, we must learn how to resist some dark forces that are hell-bent on having it lead us, ah . . . somewhere else.

As this Old Testament story goes, Sarah had already been married seven times, but, because of the work of a demon, each groom *died* before having intercourse with her (see Tobit 6:13–14). (Talk about an anticlimactic honeymoon—and seven times in a row!) Then an angel appears to Tobias and tells him that *he* is to marry Sarah. John Paul II—man of keen observation that he is—remarks that Tobias had reason to be afraid. In fact, on the day of their wedding, Sarah's father was already digging Tobias's grave (see Tobit 8:9)!

Tobias courageously faces the test. He takes Sarah as his wife, enters the bridal chamber—and lives to consummate their marriage. Why does he live? Because "during the test of the first wedding night, *love supported by prayer is revealed as stronger than death*" (TOB, p. 597). Love "is victorious because it prays" (TOB, p. 601). Take a careful look at Tobias and Sarah's prayer. It contains a short review of everything we have discussed in the TOB.

"Blessed are you, O God . . . and blessed be your holy and glorious name for ever. . . . You made Adam and gave him Eve his wife as a helper and support. You said, 'It is not good that the man should be alone; let us make a helper for him like himself.' And now, O Lord, I am not taking this sister of mine because of lust, but with sincerity. Grant that I may find mercy and grow old together with her." And she said with him, "Amen." (Tobit 8:5–8)

John Paul II describes this prayer as the spouses' "conjugal creed" (see TOB 116:2). This creed originates from the depth of love in the new spouses' hearts and expresses itself in the life-giving language of their bodies. As such, this creed serves as a precise antidote to the demon's plot to write lust into their hearts and death into their bodies. Tobias first praises God for his sheer goodness. Then, as Christ will direct us to do, he sets his heart on God's original plan for marriage. He calls Sarah "sister" like the lover in the Song of Songs. He contrasts lust with the sincere gift of self. He knows that he needs God's mercy to live the truth of love, and he longs to spend his whole life with her. Sarah's "Amen" demonstrates that she shares one and the same desire.

Tobias's love for Sarah is a "type" of Christ's love for the Church. Christ stared death in the face on the "marriage bed of the cross," thus consummating his love for the Church and conquering death by rising to new life. Tobias also stared death in the face on his marriage bed, and inspired with sacrificial (Christlike) love, he also conquered death. After seven men had succumbed, Tobias *consummates the marriage and lives!*

If sexual union is a test of life or death, then in the face of authentic spousal love, death has no chance. "Where, O death, is your victory? Where, O death, is your sting?" (1 Corinthians 15:55). Spouses who by God's grace love one another according to God's original plan—and who trust completely in God's mercy to make up for their failings, weaknesses, and sins—have no fear of this test. They are ready and willing to place themselves "between the forces of good and evil . . . because love is confident in the victory of good and is ready to do everything in order that good may conquer" (TOB 115:2).

Spousal Love as Prayer

We have already learned much about the "great mystery" spoken of in Ephesians 5. At the end of his section on marriage as a human sign of divine love, John Paul II returns to this classic text to reconfirm even more deeply the profound meaning of joining in one flesh. He observes that if the sacramental sign of marriage is based on the language of the body reread in the truth of love, then Ephesians 5 offers us the *definitive* expression of this sign reread in the truth of love.

The Song of Songs contains "'the language of the body' in all the richness of its subjective meaning" (TOB 117:2). In other words, the lovers' duet in the Song allows us in some way to enter their interior, subjective experience of love, as does the story of Tobias and Sarah. Ephesians 5, on the other hand, "contains *the 'objective' confirmation of this language* in its entirety" (TOB 117:2). There we read that the one-flesh union is a "great mystery" that is meant to express and proclaim the love of Christ and the Church. Despite what a given couple might express subjectively, Ephesians 5 presents the objective truth of the language of the body: what it is meant to express.

The internal goal (and lifelong challenge!) of every marriage is for the spouses to ensure that what they express *subjectively* in their sexual union confirms the *objective* truth of God's plan. As countless couples can attest, simply getting married is not enough to make sexual union something holy and beautiful. Marriage is the objective prerequisite to experience the true glory and holiness of sex. But the couple's *ethos*—their inner orientation and desires—must come to correspond to the true dignity of the person and the true meaning of spousal love. This, of course, calls for lifelong conversion and healing. In a word, it demands a life of deep *prayer*.

Prayer, as we observed earlier, is where we "let our masks fall and turn our hearts back to the Lord who loves us, so as to hand ourselves over to him as an offering to be purified and transformed" (*CCC*, 2711). This is precisely what Tobias and Sarah did before uniting—from within the bridal chamber, they sought the Lord in prayer: "And now, O Lord, I am not taking this sister of mine because of lust, but with sincerity. Grant that I may find mercy. . . . And Sarah said with him, 'Amen'" (Tobit 8:7–8). Here we witness *"the moment of purification"* to which spouses must submit themselves if they wish to express the spousal meaning of the body in all its truth (see TOB 116:3).

To the degree that this profound integration between objective reality and subjective experience occurs, John Paul II says that spouses experience the language of the body for what it is. They experience it as *the language of the Church's liturgy* (see TOB 116:5). This idea brings us to the pinnacle of the value John Paul II places on spousal love. Here we cross the threshold of the "great mystery" and enter into the most profound integration of the sexual and the sacred.

In the *Catechism* we learn that in the Christian tradition liturgy "means the participation of the People of God in 'the work of God'" (*CCC*, 1069). The work of God refers above all to the "great mystery" of our redemption in Christ accomplished through his death and resurrection. To say that spousal love is "liturgical" is to say that it participates in this "great mystery." The cross is where Christ consummated his marriage. Hence, as John Paul II wrote, "Spouses are . . . the permanent reminder to the Church of what happened on the cross."[91]

Liturgy is also the Church's "celebration of divine worship" (*CCC*, 1070). When lived according to the "great mystery" of God's design, the marital embrace itself becomes a profound prayer. It becomes "eucharistic"—an act of thanksgiving offered to God for the joyous gift of sharing in his life and love (*eucharist* means "thanksgiving"). According to the analogy, we can even view the marital bed as an altar upon which spouses offer their bodies in living sacrifice, holy and acceptable to God. This is their spiritual act of worship (see Romans 12:1).

If the sexual revolution of the twentieth century turned sex into an idol to be worshiped, "the Christian revolution," as I say in my book *Heaven's Song*, "transforms sex from something that is *worshiped* to something that is *worship*."[92] (HS, p. 130).

Prayer as Nuptial Union

Such a lofty vision of marital intercourse may seem hopelessly unrealistic, even undesirable to some: *Come on—sex is meant to be a prayer? Like my husband would ever go for that! Or, Who wants sex to be prayerful? What a turnoff!*

While it may be the case that a given spouse has no interest in pursuing a prayerful sex life, the above sentiments reflect tragically misinformed notions of both sex and prayer. Yes, authentic prayer not only *can* but *should* turn off lust. But authentic prayer *can* and certainly *should* turn on the noble and deep-flowing passion of genuine eros. In fact, the great mystical tradition of the Church can find no better language with which to describe prayer itself than the language of erotic love.

Prayer, from this perspective, is akin to the surrender of the bride to her bridegroom. When a Christian prays, as Pope Benedict XVI affirmed, he "tries to approach the Lord and thus seeks to enter into nuptial union with him."[93] This means we must have the courage to "get naked" before God (remove the fig leaves, take our masks off) so that the heavenly Bridegroom can enter our hearts and love us *freely, totally, faithfully*, and *fruitfully*. "According to the words of Sacred Scripture," wrote John Paul II, "God penetrates the creature, who is completely 'naked' before him" (TOB 12:5, note 22).

What we are learning in the TOB is that only to the degree that we are living in nuptial union with God are we capable of living in authentic nuptial union with an earthly spouse. This is what joining in one flesh is: a sacramental sign of union with God. Could there possibly be a more exalted notion of sexual union than to see it as a sign of union with God?

Imaging God's Love

If the lovers of the Song of Songs proclaim the joy of living the true sign of marital love while Tobias and Sarah face a life-or-death test to reclaim the truth of that sign, what light does this shed on the Church's teaching on sexual morality?

Ultimately, all questions of sexual morality come down to one very simple question: Does what we're doing with our bodies truly image God's *free, total, faithful, fruitful* love or does it miss the mark? If it misses the mark, is the solution to adjust the target, or to adjust our aim?

Think of it this way: If sexual intercourse is meant to be a renewal of wedding vows, how healthy would a marriage be if spouses were regularly unfaithful to their vows? On the other hand, how healthy would a marriage be if spouses regularly renewed their vows, expressing an ever-increasing commitment to them? As we will see more clearly in the next chapter, this is precisely what is at stake in the Church's teaching on sexual morality.

But it's not up to us to try really hard to love as God loves. On our own, *we simply cannot do it.* As Pope Francis affirms, we mustn't "lay upon two limited persons the tremendous burden of having to reproduce perfectly the union between Christ and his Church." Rather, we must invite men and women to open to God's transforming grace, "for marriage as a sign . . . advances gradually with the progressive integration of the gifts of God."[94] "The language of the body calls for a patient apprenticeship in learning to interpret and channel desires in view of authentic self-giving."[95]

This patient apprenticeship progresses to the degree that we remain open to the gift of his love poured into our hearts. "God's love has been poured into our hearts through the Holy Spirit who has been given to us" (Romans 5:5). A life of deep prayer and frequent reception of the sacraments is what opens us to the divine gift of love, like a bride opening to the gift of her bridegroom. Continually receiving so great a gift, we are enabled to share that love with others in ever deepening ways. This is the only context in which we can properly understand the authentically Christian vision of sexuality.

FOR REFLECTION

1. According the TOB, how does marital intercourse express and communicate the "great mystery" of divine love?

2. How does understanding St. John Paul's teaching enable you to live out your own calling (whether married, single, or consecrated celibate) more fully and fruitfully?

3. What new insights do you have about the Bible and God's plan of salvation having learned more about the erotic love poetry of the Song of Songs and the liturgical prayer of Tobias and Sarah?

Thank you, God, for giving St. John Paul II the wisdom and understanding contained in Theology of the Body. Through his teachings, we come to see that your plan for making us in your image and likeness is more glorious than we could ever have imagined. Help us to respect the gift of our creation as male and female and live it to your glory. Amen.

EIGHT

Theology in the Bedroom

Every man and every woman fully realizes himself or herself through
the sincere gift of self. For spouses, the moment of conjugal union constitutes
a very particular expression of this.

—St. John Paul II

Can you think of a time in your life when your heart was pierced by something so beautiful that it made you ache inside because of it? On a recent trip to British Columbia, just east of Vancouver, I was overwhelmed at the sight of Cascade Falls—crystal-clear glacial waters falling from several stories high into emerald pools surrounded by towering cedars and water-worn rock walls. My heart leaped at the sight. And I was filled with a painful longing, a kind of nostalgia that grabbed me in the chest and became a prayer, lifting me up into the realm of something mysterious, something otherworldly.

There is "a kind of salvation which occurs in beauty and in those who behold it," observes Pope Francis.[96] It was this salvation to which the elderly priest was inviting the young couple under the stars. From what did they need to be saved? They needed to be saved, as we all do, from the danger of human desire turned in on itself, from the futility of aiming our desire for the infinite at something finite. Small "b" beauty is meant to launch us to capital "B" Beauty, as we've been learning. But when we aim our desire for capital "B" Beauty at small "b" beauty, we miss the mark. We sin. Only in this context—the context of our God-given longing to participate in infinite Beauty—does the Church's moral teaching take on its true meaning.

Pope Francis has spoken repeatedly about the serious problem involved when "certain issues which are part of the Church's moral teaching are taken out of the context which gives them their meaning." When we speak of specific and often controversial moral questions, it's necessary to help our audience understand "the full background to what we are saying" so that they are capable of relating the Church's moral teaching "to the very heart of the Gospel which gives it meaning, beauty, and attractiveness."[97] This is precisely what we have been doing throughout this book: giving "the full background" to the Church's teaching on sexual morality; rescuing that teaching from a judgmental moralism and restoring to it the "freshness and fragrance of the Gospel."[98]

Embracing Our Greatness

Perhaps at this point you're feeling some trepidation. You have understood St. John Paul II's logic, you can see where it's headed, and you know your life doesn't measure up. Welcome to the human race. The good news is that Christ can restore us to the full measure of our humanity. Remember—Christ has "come to 'save' the world, beginning from eros."[99] There is "new wine" poured out for us. We need only open our hearts to this "wine" and allow it in to do its healing, transforming work. It doesn't matter where you've been or what mistakes you've made. The TOB is a message of salvation, not condemnation.

"Christian morality is not a titanic effort of the will, the effort of someone who decides to be consistent and succeeds," says Pope Francis. "No. Christian morality is . . . the heartfelt response to [the] surprising, unforeseeable, 'unjust' mercy . . . of one who knows me, knows my betrayals and loves me just the same, appreciates me, embraces me, calls me again, hopes in me, and expects from me. This is why the Christian conception of morality is a revolution," concludes Francis, "it is not a never falling down but an always getting up again."[100]

Authentic Christian morality is not against us. It is unstintingly *for* us. The first line in the *Catechism's* section on "Life in Christ" speaks volumes. It doesn't say, "Give up everything you really want and follow all these miserable rules or you're going to hell." It says, "Christian, recognize your dignity" (*CCC*, 1691). This is what John Paul II's TOB has been proclaiming all along—our dignity, our greatness as male and female. This dignity and greatness rests above all on the fact that we are called to communion with God (see *CCC*, 27). And *that* is what the communion of man and woman is meant to signify. It is the sacrament of eternal communion with God. Now it's time to follow these stupendous truths to their logical conclusion.

If we are to accept our dignity, our greatness, we must also accept the demands it makes on us. At times those demands can feel incredibly burdensome. And yet Jesus insists that his yoke is "easy" and his burden "light" (Matthew 11:30). And John the Evangelist insists that "his commandments are not burdensome" (1 John 5:3). If they *feel* burdensome, it's probably because we're relying on our own strength to carry them out. As John Paul II said plainly, what the Gospel demands of us "is beyond man's abilities." Living the love we're called to is "possible only as a result of a gift of God who heals, restores, and transforms the human heart by his grace."[101]

The beautiful and simple truth of our sexuality is this: We are called to love as God loves, through the "sincere gift of self." And the good news of the Gospel is that "God's love has been poured into our hearts by the Holy Spirit who has been given to us" (Romans 5:5). This, says John Paul II, "is the essential and fundamental 'power' [to live according to the demands of our own greatness]: *the love planted in the heart . . . by the Holy Spirit.*" Through prayer and the sacraments, "that essential and *creative spiritual 'power' of love* reaches human hearts and, at the same time, human bodies in their subjective masculinity and femininity" (TOB 126:5).

No, God does not make impossible demands on us. "He simply asks that we sincerely look at our life and present ourselves honestly before him," says Pope Francis, "and that we be willing to continue to grow, asking from him what we ourselves cannot as yet achieve."[102] With utmost confidence in God's patient mercy and love, let's take a look at what it means to speak the language of sexual love honestly.

Applying the Basic Principle

At the close of the last chapter, I observed that all questions of sexual morality ultimately come down to one: Does what we're doing with our bodies truly image God's *free, total, faithful, fruitful* love or does it miss the mark? My book *Good News about Sex &*

THEOLOGY OF THE BODY • 181

Marriage uses this principle to answer 115 of the most common questions and objections to Church teaching. I refer you to that for a more detailed discussion. For now, we'll just apply the principle to a few specific questions with the aim of arriving at the core of sexual morality.

Before we do, however, it's critical that we hold God's hands of mercy. Without grounding ourselves there, we will be tempted either to despair over our sin or to rationalize it away. If God's mercy and forgiveness are real, we should never fear to acknowledge where we have missed the mark. The only sin we should fear, in fact, is the rationalization of sin—the refusal to acknowledge sin as sin. Such obstinacy involves the blaspheming of the Holy Spirit that Jesus referred to as the "unforgivable sin" (see Matthew 12:32). It's unforgivable because it's unrepentant. So, if we discover we have missed the mark, let us be repentant, go to confession, and entrust ourselves to God's mercy. Only from that secure place of trust in God's mercy can we look honestly at sin without despairing or rationalizing. Here we go.

Does an act of masturbation image God's *free, total, faithful, fruitful* love or does it miss the mark? Does an act of fornication (sex between two unmarried people) image God's *free, total, faithful, fruitful* love or does it miss the mark? What about an act of adultery? What about homosexual behavior? What about lusting after pornographic images? And here is where the rubber hits the road (pun intended): Does an intentionally sterilized act of intercourse image God's *free, total, faithful, fruitful* love or does it miss the mark?

If you find yourself resisting the logical conclusion to the above questions, recall what we said previously: Perhaps the problem is not with the teaching of the Church; perhaps the problem is exactly what Jesus indicated it was—our own "hardness of heart" (Matthew 19:8). If today you hear his voice . . . harden not your hearts (see Hebrews 3:15).

Sex and Marriage Redefined

Catholic teaching on these matters can be summarized quite succinctly: marriage, sex, and babies belong together . . . and in that order. In his loving and beautiful design, God has united these three realities in a tight knot to reveal in our flesh the truth of his own eternal covenant love and Fatherhood. Sexual sin, in one way or another, always seeks to untie this knot, to separate what God has joined. It's an attempt to grasp at the pleasure of genital activity apart from the God-given purpose of genital activity: communion and generation in the image of God.

Wise men and women throughout history (not just Catholics) have recognized that respect for the generative power of our genitals is the linchpin of all sexual morality. Even Sigmund Freud understood this. He wrote that the "abandonment of the reproductive function is the common feature of all perversions. We actually describe a sexual activity as perverse if it has given up the aim of reproduction and pursues the attainment of pleasure as an aim independent of it."[103]

Consider this: When we divorce sex from its natural orientation toward new life, what is left to prevent the justification of any and every means to sexual climax? When we deliberately sterilize sex, we fundamentally disorient the act. It no longer points of necessity to marriage and the raising of a family. Indulging libido for its own sake becomes the name of the game, and we eventually treat natural, vaginal intercourse as only one of a million and one ways to do that. When we pry sex loose from its most natural consequence, we inevitably lose our moral compass. Welcome to the world in which we live.

The monogamous, lifelong union of the sexes and the family that results has served as the bedrock of civilization for centuries. Yet during the twentieth century, in only a few generations, sex, marriage, and the family were radically deconstructed and redefined. Behaviors once commonly recognized as an affront to human dignity and a serious threat to the social order are now not only touted by the media as harmless pleasures to be prized and pursued; they're also sanctioned and protected as legal "rights" by the government.

Have you ever wondered what brought about so radical a shift so quickly? The answer is complex, but one thing is certain: If the modern brand of sexual "liberation" was to flourish, the natural consequence of sex (procreation) *had* to be eliminated. The sexual revolution of the twentieth century is simply inexplicable apart from the nearly universal acceptance of contraception.

Proponents of contraception in the early 1900s knew that advancing their cause would be impossible without the "blessing" of Christian leaders. It's a little-known fact that until 1930, Catholics, Orthodox, and Protestants stood together in their condemnation of any attempt to deliberately sterilize the marital act. That year, the Anglican Church broke with more than 1,900 years of uninterrupted Christian teaching. When the Pill debuted in the early 1960s, the Catholic Church was the only Christian body retaining what in thirty short years had come to be seen as an archaic, even absurd position.

Inspired by a widespread but faulty view of the Second Vatican Council, many expected that a papal blessing of contraception was imminent. Withstanding unimaginable global pressure, Pope Paul VI shocked the world when he reaffirmed the traditional teaching against contraception in his 1968 encyclical letter *Humanae Vitae (Of Human Life)*. It fell like a bomb. The widespread dissent that immediately followed has not ceased to this day.

We Need a "Total Vision of Man"

Was Paul VI hopelessly out of touch with reality? Or maybe—just maybe—was he speaking a difficult, yet unchangeable truth to a world blinded by its excesses and lusts? If you have resisted the Church's teaching on contraception, believe me, I can relate. In fact, I almost left the Catholic Church because of this "blasted teaching." *Give me a break*, I thought. *Denying people contraception is like denying people toothpaste or toilet paper. It's just another modern convenience. What's the big deal?*

Paul VI knew it would be difficult for the modern world to understand the immorality of contraception. Modern men and women had lost sight of the greatness, dignity, and divine purpose *of human life*. When that happens, we no longer see the sexual union as a "great mystery" proclaiming God's love for humanity and foreshadowing heaven. We quickly reduce sex merely to a biological process subject to all sorts of human manipulations. Today, because of this mind-set, most men and women give no more thought to tinkering with their fertility than they do to tinkering with their hair color.

Sex is certainly biological, but that's only a partial perspective. As Paul VI observed, in order to understand Christian teaching on sex and procreation, we must look "beyond partial perspectives" to a "total vision of man and of his vocation."[104] This is what John Paul II set out to do in his Theology of the Body—provide the "total vision of man" that would enable us to understand the Church's teaching on contraception. In fact, John Paul II says that the entire TOB can be considered *an extensive commentary* on the doctrine contained precisely in *Humanae Vitae*" (TOB 133:2). Again, I think of Pope Francis insisting that we speak of sexual matters in the overall biblical context that gives them their true meaning, beauty, and attractiveness: *That's* what the TOB is.

All of our preceding reflections have led us to this point. If I have successfully introduced you to John Paul II's beautiful vision of the human person, the basic logic of *Humanae Vitae* should be fairly clear. But important questions raised by Paul VI's encyclical still remain. What particular insight does John Paul II's TOB offer us in understanding *Humanae Vitae*? Why does the Church reject contraception but accept natural methods of regulating fertility? What does the Church mean by the practice of "responsible parenthood"? Doesn't the Church's teaching against contraception impede couples from expressing their love for one another? Let's take a closer look. And remember: Be not afraid! The truth is not afraid of our questions. The question is, are we afraid of the truth? There is no need to be. It is the truth—and only the truth—that can set us free to love.

Ethics of the Sign

As John Paul II observes, the teaching of *Humanae Vitae* "is strictly linked with our earlier reflections about *marriage in the dimension of the (sacramental) sign*" (TOB 118:3). We can argue against contraception with philosophical reasoning alone, without any appeal to faith or the Bible. But John Paul II's project was to show the deepest *theological* reason for the immorality of contraception. Here it is: Rendering the one-flesh union sterile falsifies the sacramental sign of married love. It violates what John Paul II calls the ethics of the sign.

As a sacrament, marriage not only signifies God's life and love, it *really participates* in God's life and love—or, at least, it's meant to do so. For sacraments to convey grace (God's life and love), the sacramental sign must accurately signify the spiritual mystery. For example, as we mentioned in the last chapter, as a physical sign of cleansing, the waters of baptism really and truly bring about a spiritual cleansing from sin. But if you were to baptize someone with mud or tar, no spiritual cleansing would take place because the physical sign is now one of making someone dirty. This would actually be a counter-sign of the spiritual reality of baptism.

All of married life is a sacrament. All of married life is meant to be a sign of God's life and love. But this sacrament has a consummate expression. Sexual intercourse is the full-bodied sign language of God's love. Here, like no other moment in married life, spouses are invited to participate in the "great mystery" of God's creative and redemptive love. But this will only happen if their sexual union accurately *signifies* God's love. Therefore, as John Paul II concludes, we can speak of moral good and evil in the sexual relationship based on whether the couple gives to their union "the character of a truthful sign" (TOB 37:6).

The essential element for marriage to be a "true sign"—an authentic "sacrament"—is the language of the body spoken in truth. This is precisely how spouses "constitute" the sacramental sign of marriage (see TOB 104:9). By participating in God's eternal plan of love, the language of the body becomes "prophetic." As John Paul II observes, the teaching of *Humanae Vitae* simply carries this truth to its logical conclusions (see TOB 123:2).

Insert contraception into the language of the body and (knowingly or unknowingly) the couple engages in a *counter-sign* of the "great mystery." Rather than proclaiming, "God is life-giving love," the language of contracepted intercourse says, "God is *not* life-giving love." In this way spouses (knowingly or unknowingly) become "false prophets." They blaspheme. Their bodies are still proclaiming a "theology," but it's a false theology, a false image of God.

If the Church's vision of what it means to be human is correct, then contraception is a cunning betrayal of the deepest truth of our humanity. In fact, if the Church's vision of what it means to be human is correct, we can only conclude that contracepted sex denies and attacks at its roots our creation in the image of God.

Fidelity to the Wedding Vows

Pope Francis observes that the "Gospel tells us to correct others and to help them grow on the basis of a recognition of the objective evil of their actions (see Matthew 18:15), but without making judgments about their responsibility and culpability (see Matthew 7:1; Luke 6:37)."[105] Case in point: Most couples who use contraception simply have no idea what they are doing or saying with their bodies. They haven't ever heard or understood the "great mystery" of their sexuality. Hence, the conclusions we're drawing here about the objective seriousness of contraception is not a matter of assigning culpability.

That said, even if a couple's ignorance makes them subjectively innocent in this regard, contraception will still have its damaging effect on their relationship. For example, if I drink a cup of poison, but don't know it's poison, I haven't committed suicide; I'm not culpable for my own death. But it will still kill me, since whether or not I *think* it's poison has no bearing whatsoever on whether or not it *is* poison.

If we open our eyes, we can see the effects of contraception's "poison" everywhere in our world today. The main goal of sex in a contracepting world is not the expression of the marital commitment and the raising of a family; the main goal of sex in such a world is pleasure. And, as we observed in chapter one, when pleasure is the main goal of sex, society becomes utilitarian. You are valued if you're useful, and you're useful if you bring me pleasure. If you don't, or if you cease to, you'll be ignored, rejected, abandoned, possibly even exterminated. And here we catch a glimpse of the role contraception plays in a "culture of death," where people are not loved and cherished as *subjects*, but used and discarded as *objects*.

The causes of the dramatic rise in divorce in our culture are multiple and complex. Still, it should not surprise us in the least that the spike in divorce has coincided with the acceptance and practice of contraception. What's the connection? In short, as I asked in the last chapter, how healthy would a marriage be if a husband and wife were regularly unfaithful to their wedding vows? Sexual intercourse is meant to renew and express wedding vows. But contraception turns the "I do" of those vows into an "I do not."

During conjugal intercourse, a *"moment so rich in meaning,* it is . . . particularly important that the 'language of the body' be re-read in truth" (TOB 118:4). We are free to choose whether to engage in sex. But if we choose to engage in sex, we are not free to change its meaning. The language of the body has "clear-cut meanings," all of which are "programmed," John Paul II says, in the conjugal consent, in the vows. For example, to "the question: 'Are you ready to accept children lovingly from God? . . .' the man and the woman answer, 'Yes'" (TOB 105:6, 106:3).

If spouses say "yes" at the altar, but then render their union sterile, they are lying with their bodies. They are being unfaithful to their wedding vows. Such dishonesty at the heart of the marital covenant cannot fail to have a deleterious effect on the couple's relationship. Fertility is not an afterthought in God's design for marital love. Rather, it "is present from the beginning of love as an essential feature, one that cannot be denied without disfiguring that love itself," observes Pope Francis. "Hence no genital act of husband and wife can refuse this meaning."[106]

Someone might retort, "Come on! I can commit to being 'open to children' at the altar, but this doesn't mean that *each* and *every* act of intercourse needs to be open to children." But that makes as much sense as saying, "Come on! I can commit to fidelity at the altar, but this doesn't mean that *each* and *every* act of intercourse needs to be with my spouse." If you can recognize the inconsistency of a commitment to fidelity, *but not always* . . . you can recognize the inconsistency of a commitment to being open to children, *but not always*.

Perhaps another way out of this logic is simply for a couple to exclude openness to children in the commitment they make at the altar. Then a couple wouldn't be lying with their bodies by using contraception, would they? It would reflect what they committed to, yes. But what they committed to would not be to love as God loves. What they committed to would not be marriage. Indeed, as the Church has always recognized, willfully excluding openness to children renders a marriage null from the start.

Responsible Parenthood

So, does fidelity to the wedding vows imply that couples are to leave the number of children they have entirely to chance? No. In calling couples to a responsible love, the Church calls them also to a responsible parenthood.

Paul VI stated clearly that couples are considered "to exercise responsible parenthood who prudently and generously decide to have a large family, or who, for serious reasons and with due respect to the moral law, choose to have no more children for the time being or even for an indeterminate period."[107] Notice that large families should result from prudent reflection and generosity, not chance. Notice, too, that couples must have "serious reasons" to avoid pregnancy and must respect the moral law, the ethics of the sign.

Assuming a couple has a serious reason to avoid a child (this could be financial, physical, or psychological, among other reasons), what could they do that would not violate the consummate expression of their sacrament? In other words, what could they do to avoid conceiving a child that would not render them unfaithful to their wedding vows? I'll bet you a million dollars you're doing it right now. They could *abstain* from sex. If we understand the dignity of the human being and the astounding meaning of becoming one flesh, we will logically conclude, as the Church always has, that the only method of "birth control" in keeping with human dignity is self-control.

A further question arises: Would a couple be doing anything to falsify their sexual union if they embraced during a time of natural infertility? Take, for example, a couple past childbearing years. They know their union will not result in a child. Are they violating the sacramental sign of their marriage if they engage in intercourse with this knowledge? Are they contracepting? No. Contraception, by definition, is the choice to engage in an act of intercourse, but then do something else to *render* it sterile. This can be done by using various devices, hormones, surgical procedures, and the age-old method of withdrawal (*coitus interruptus*).

Couples who use natural family planning (NFP) when they have a just reason to avoid pregnancy *never* render their sexual acts sterile; they never contracept. They track their fertility, abstain when they are fertile and, if they so desire, embrace when they are naturally infertile. Readers unfamiliar with modern NFP methods should note that they are 98 to 99 percent effective at avoiding pregnancy when used properly. Furthermore, any woman, regardless of the regularity of her cycles, can use NFP successfully. This is not the outdated and much less precise "rhythm method."

What's the Difference?

To some people this seems like splitting hairs. "What's the big difference," they ask, "between rendering the union sterile yourself and just *waiting* until it's naturally infertile? The end result is the same thing: both couples avoid children." To which I respond, "What's the big difference between killing Grandma and just *waiting* until she dies naturally? The end result is the same thing: dead Grandma." Yes, the end result is the same thing, but one case involves a serious sin called murder, while in the other case, Grandma dies, but there's no sin involved. Give it some thought: If you can understand the difference between euthanasia and natural death, you can understand the difference between contraception and natural family planning.

John Paul II rightly observes that the difference between periodic abstinence (NFP) and contraception "is much wider and deeper than is usually thought, one which involves in the final analysis two irreconcilable concepts of the human person and of human sexuality."[108] The difference, in fact, is one of cosmic proportions.

First, it's important to realize that the Church has never said it is inherently wrong to avoid children. But the end (avoiding children) does not justify the means. There may well be a good reason for you to wish Grandma would pass on to the next life. Perhaps she is suffering terribly with age and disease. But this does not justify killing her. Similarly, you may have a good reason to avoid conceiving a child. Perhaps you are in serious financial straits. Perhaps you have four kids under the age of four and you have reached your emotional limits. But no scenario justifies rendering the sexual act sterile, just as no scenario justifies killing Grandma.

Grandma's natural death and a woman's natural period of infertility are both acts of God. But in killing Grandma or in rendering sex sterile, we take the powers of life *into our own hands*—just like the deceiver originally tempted us to do—and we make ourselves like God (see Genesis 3:5). Therefore, as John Paul II concludes, "Contraception is to be judged so profoundly unlawful as never to be, for any reason, justified. To think or to say the contrary is equal to maintaining that in human life, situations may arise in which it is lawful not to recognize God as God."[109]

Love or Lust?

One of the main objections to *Humanae Vitae* is that following its teaching (that is, practicing periodic abstinence when avoiding pregnancy) impedes couples from expressing their love for one another. Let's take a closer look at this objection.

First of all, it is true that abstaining from sex for the wrong reasons (out of spite for a spouse, or out of disdain for sex, for example) is damaging to marital love. But, as every married couples knows, abstaining from sex for the right reasons can be a profound act of love. Indeed, there are many occasions in married life when a couple might *want* to renew their vows through intercourse, but love demands they abstain: Maybe one of the spouses is sick; maybe it's after childbirth; maybe they're at the in-laws and there are thin walls; or maybe the couple has a serious reason to avoid a child. In these cases, and in many others, if a couple can't abstain, their love is called into question.

God is the one who united marital love and procreation. Therefore, since God cannot contradict himself, a "true contradiction cannot exist between the divine laws pertaining to the transmission of life and those pertaining to the fostering of authentic conjugal love."[110] It may well be difficult to follow the teaching of *Humanae Vitae*, but it could never be a contradiction of love.

Following this teaching is difficult because of the internal battle we all experience between love and lust (true eros and the distortions thereof). Lust impels us, and impels us very powerfully, toward sexual activity. However, if this activity results from nothing more than a desire we can't control, it's not love we're expressing; it's love's opposite: use. In reality, what we often call love, "if subjected to searching critical examination turns out to be, contrary to all appearances, only a form of 'utilization' of the person[111]"

What purpose does contraception really serve? This might sound odd at first, but let it sink in. Contraception was not invented to prevent pregnancy. We already had a 100 percent safe, 100 percent reliable way of doing that—*abstinence*. In the final analysis, contraception serves one purpose: to spare us the difficulty we experience when confronted with the choice of abstinence. When all the smoke is cleared, contraception was invented because of our lack of self-control; in other words, contraception was invented to serve the indulgence of lust.

Why do we spay or neuter our dogs and cats? Why don't we just ask them to abstain? Because they cannot say no to their urge to merge; they're not free. If we spay and neuter ourselves through contraceptive practices, we are reducing the "great mystery" of the one-flesh union to the level of Fido and Fidette in heat. What distinguished us from the animals in the first place (remember original solitude)? *Freedom!* God gave us freedom as the capacity to love. Contraception negates this freedom. It says, "I can't abstain." Hence, contracepted intercourse not only attacks the procreative meaning of sex, "it also *ceases to be an act of love*" (TOB 123:6). If you cannot say "no" to sex, what does your "yes" mean? Only the person who is *free* with the freedom for which Christ set us free (see Galatians 5:1) is capable of authentic love.

Paraphrasing insights from Dr. Greg Popcak, we need to recognize that any frustration we feel in practicing the abstinence required of NFP is a sign that NFP is doing the job it's meant to do: helping us grow in virtue. When we feel those frustrations, we must learn to recognize them as the growing pains of personal maturity and the capacity for expressing authentic love. In those times when the growing pains hurt the most, we're not feeling a sexual urge that must be satisfied, but a selfish urge that must be transformed if we are to reclaim the freedom that our fallenness has taken from us. This is the gift and role of true chastity.

Chastity and the Integration of Love

Chastity, so often considered "negative" or "repressive," is supremely positive and liberating. It's the virtue that frees sexual desire from the utilitarian attitude, from the tendency to *use* others for our own gratification. Chastity requires "an *apprenticeship in self-mastery* which is training in human freedom. The alternative is clear: either man governs his passions and finds peace, or he lets himself be dominated by them and becomes unhappy" (CCC, 2339).

As we learned in chapter three, self-mastery does not merely mean resisting unruly desires by force of will. That's only the negative side of the picture. As we develop self-mastery, we experience it as "*the ability to orient* [sexual] reactions, both as to their content and as to their character" (TOB 129:5). The person who is truly chaste is able to direct erotic desire "toward what is true, good, and beautiful, so that what is 'erotic' also becomes true, good, and beautiful" (TOB 48:1). As spouses experience liberation from lust, they enter into the freedom of the gift, which enables them to express the language of their bodies "in a depth, simplicity, and beauty hitherto altogether unknown" (TOB 117b:5).

It's certainly true that chastity requires "asceticism," understood as a ready and determined willingness to resist the impulses of lust. But, remember, authentic chastity does not repress. It enters into Christ's death and resurrection. As lust dies, authentic love is raised up. As John Paul II expresses it, "If conjugal chastity (and chastity in general) manifests itself at first as an ability to resist [lust], it subsequently reveals itself as a *singular ability* to perceive, love, and realize those meanings of the 'language of the body' that remain completely unknown to [lust] itself" (TOB 128:3). Hence, the discipline required by chastity does not impoverish or impede a couple's expressions of love and affection. Rather, "it makes them spiritually more intense and thus *enriches* them" (TOB 128:3).

Marital Spirituality

Such chastity, John Paul II says, stands at the center of the spirituality of marriage (see TOB 131:2). What is marital spirituality? It's living according to God's inspiration in married life. It involves spouses opening themselves to the indwelling power of the Holy Spirit and allowing him to guide them in all their choices and behaviors. John Paul II says that sexual union itself—with all its emotional joys and physical pleasures—is meant to be an expression of "life according to the Holy Spirit" (see TOB 101:6). When spouses are open to the gift, the Holy Spirit infuses them "with everything that is noble and beautiful," with "the supreme value which is love" (TOB 46:5). But when spouses close themselves off to the Holy Spirit, sexual union quickly degenerates into an act of mutual exploitation.

Without the Holy Spirit, human weakness makes the teaching of *Humanae Vitae* a burden no one can bear. But to whom is this teaching given? To men and women enslaved by their weaknesses? Or to men and women set free by the *power* of the Holy Spirit? This is what is at stake in the teaching of *Humanae Vitae*—the power of the Gospel! The Church holds out the teaching of *Humanae Vitae* with absolute confidence in the fact that "God's love has been poured into our hearts by the Holy Spirit who has been given to us" (Romans 5:5).

Married couples "must implore [God] for such 'power' and for every other divine help in prayer . . . they must draw grace and love from the ever-living fountain of the Eucharist; . . . 'with humble perseverance' they must overcome their own faults and sins in the sacrament of Penance. These are the means—*infallible and indispensable*—to form the Christian spirituality of conjugal . . . life" (TOB 126:5). All of which, of course, presupposes faith, that openness of the human heart to the gift of the Holy Spirit.

If spouses are not living an authentic spirituality—in other words, if their hearts aren't open to the transforming power of the Holy Spirit—they will tend to view the Church's teaching against contraception as an oppressive rule imposed by an oppressive Church. On the other hand, spouses who engage in their sexual embrace as an expression of life according to the Holy Spirit recognize the Church's teaching as the path to the love and freedom for which they yearn. In turn, they are filled with a profound reverence for what comes from God, which shapes their spirituality *"for the sake of protecting the particular dignity of [the sexual] act"* (TOB 132:2). Such spouses understand that their union is meant to signify and participate in God's creative and redeeming love. In other words, they understand the theology of their bodies. And being filled with a deep "veneration for *the essential values of conjugal union"* saves them from "violating or degrading what bears in itself the sign of the divine mystery of creation and redemption" (TOB 131:5).

Getting to this place of freely and joyfully embracing the divine plan for sexual love can be a long journey, of course. As Pope Francis states, "Reaching a level of maturity where individuals can make truly free and responsible decisions calls for much time and patience."[112] But this vision of marital spirituality *can* become a lived reality in a couple's life as they allow grace into the inner recesses of their hearts.

The Antithesis of Marital Spirituality

John Paul II observes that life in the Holy Spirit leads couples to understand, among all the possible manifestations of love and affection, "the singular, and even exceptional meaning" of the sexual embrace (TOB 132:2). However, contraceptive practice—and the mentality behind it—demonstrates a serious lack of understanding of the exceptional significance of the sexual embrace in God's plan. Such a lack, he says, constitutes in a way the antithesis of marital spirituality (see TOB 132:2). How so?

If marital spirituality involves spouses opening their bodies—and the one body they become in the sexual act—to the Holy Spirit, contraception marks a specific closing off of their bodies to the Holy Spirit. Who is the Holy Spirit? As we say in the Nicene Creed, he is "the Lord, the Giver of Life." What does contracepted sex say, if not: "Lord and Giver of Life, we don't want you to be part of this act"?

If sexual union is meant to enable us to participate in God's eternal exchange of love, do you know what couples actually say with their bodies when they close their union to the Lord and Giver of Life? In short, whether they realize this or not, contracepted intercourse says, "We prefer the momentary pleasure of a sterilized orgasm over the opportunity of participating in the eternal ecstasy and bliss of the Trinity." To which I respond, *"Bad choice!"* But do you think if couples really knew they were choosing this, they would continue to do so? I cannot help but think of Christ's words from the cross: "Father, forgive them; for they know not what they do" (Luke 23:34).

There is no tragedy in admitting we have sinned. There is no tragedy in admitting we have been duped by a counterfeit and sold a "Pill" of goods. The only tragedy is the hardness of heart that refuses to admit its own sin. Be not afraid! As we have said so many times throughout this book, Christ came not to condemn but to save (see John 3:17). It doesn't matter how much lust has dominated our lives. It doesn't matter how "dyslexic" or even "illiterate" we may have been in reading the divine language of the body up to this point in our lives. As John Paul II boldly proclaims, through the gift of redemption "there is always the possibility of passing from 'error' to the 'truth' . . . the possibility of . . . conversion from sin to chastity as an expression of a life according to the Spirit" (TOB 107:3).

FOR REFLECTION

_____

1. Do you experience the Church's teaching on sexual morality as a burden, or as the truth that sets you free to love? In what areas do you struggle to live a moral life? Where do you see yourself trying to live God's commands in your own strength?

2. What are some of the wrong reasons a couple might abstain from sex? Explain how abstaining from sex for the right reasons can be a profound act of love. What are some of those right reasons?

3. How would you explain the difference between contraception and Natural Family Planning to someone who sees no distinction?

Come, Holy Spirit, come! Convert our hearts from lust to love.
Impregnate our sexual desires with divine passion so that, loving as
God loves on earth, we might one day rejoice in the consummation of
the "marriage of the Lamb" in heaven. Amen.

CONCLUSION

At the core of [the] Gospel . . . is the affirmation of the inseparable connection between the person, his life and his bodiliness.
—*St. John Paul II*

"And the Word became flesh and dwelt among us" (John 1:14). "Word" doesn't quite convey all the richness of the Greek *Logos. Logos* refers to the rational principle governing the universe— the ultimate "meaning," "reason," "logic" behind *everything.* The astounding claim upon which all of Christianity is based is that that Meaning has communicated itself by taking on *flesh.* . . . We've done nothing other in this study of Sacred Scripture than examine how the Incarnation illuminates our own incarnate humanity as male and female. The enfleshment of Ultimate Meaning becomes the ultimate en-meaning-ment of the flesh. It is this: to reveal, communicate, and enable us to "become partakers of the divine nature" (2 Peter 1:4).

Human flesh—yours and mine—conveys not only *a* word from God, but *the* Word *of* God: "And the Word became flesh and dwelt among us" (John 1:14). This is why our bodies, as we have learned throughout this study of God's Word, are not only *bio*-logical but *theo*-logical: They reveal the logic of God, the *Logos* of God . . . they reveal, proclaim, communicate the Word of God. Indeed, our bodies proclaim the Gospel of Jesus Christ which is *always* "the Gospel of the body" . . . the Gospel of the Word, the *Logos* (ultimate Meaning) made flesh.

Much is at stake in the rampant confusion, both in the secular world and in our churches, about the meaning of the body, sexuality, gender, marriage, and the family. As one of my theological mentors, the late Monsignor Lorenzo Albacete, observed:

> When [the Gospel] is lacking in a person or in a culture, the barometer where its lack is most clearly seen is the attitude towards the body. . . . Indeed, . . . it is the desperate confusion and disarray with respect to human bodiliness, as shown in human sexuality, that shows the need for evangelization. . . . This absolutely inseparable relation between the Gospel and the experience of the body . . . can be seen in the fact that from the very beginning the *greatest* enemy of the Gospel has been the attempt to separate Jesus Christ from the flesh [see 2 John 1:7] . . . The whole heart, the scandal, the newness, the *stunning* wonder of the Christian proposal . . . is that the Word—the Logos, Meaning, Sense, Beauty, Truth, Goodness, Destiny—has become flesh. The person who accepts [this] . . . knows that an attack against the body . . . is an attack against the very secret of God's life. And so that person develops a passion, a passion to come to the help of suffering bodies. . . . That sensitivity is in the end the decisive proof that evangelization has occurred.[113]

This suffering abounds in our post–sexual revolution world. If the essential goal of the sexual revolution was to sever the natural link between gender and the generation of human life, the goal now is to sever the natural link between human life and gender itself. Despite all claims of "liberation" and the supposed triumph of "human rights," a de-gendered world can only degenerate.

Both steps, both ruptures in our humanity—the rupture of gender from life and the rupture of life from gender—are rooted in a "new Manichaeism" in which body and soul are put in radical opposition. Severed from spiritual reality, we no longer experience the body, sexuality, and fertility as a "great mystery." Instead, we come to experience them as a "great misery." In turn, we no longer experience gender (recall that gender means "the manner in which one is designed to generate") as something to revere, but as something to reject.

When we fail to appreciate the profound unity of body and soul, we no longer see the human body in light of our creation in the image and likeness of God. Rather, we reduce it to a thing to be used, exploited, manipulated, and even discarded at will, forgetting that that body is not just "a body" but *some*-body. Within this milieu, as John Paul II observed, the human being *"ceases to live as a person and a subject.* Regardless of all intentions and declarations to the contrary, he becomes merely an *object."* Tragically, he continues:

[We have lost] the basis of that *primordial wonder* which led Adam on the morning of creation to exclaim before Eve: "This at last is bone of my bones and flesh of my flesh" (Genesis 2:23). This same wonder is echoed in the words of the Song of Songs: "You have ravished my heart, my sister, my bride, you have ravished my heart with a glance of your eyes" (Song of Songs 4:9). How far removed are some modern ideas from the profound understanding of masculinity and femininity found in divine revelation! Revelation leads us to discover in *human sexuality a treasure proper to the person*, who finds true fulfillment in [marriage and] the family but who can likewise express his profound calling . . . in celibacy for the sake of the kingdom of God.[114]

We are living in dark times indeed, but let us never forget that "the light shines in the darkness and the darkness has not overcome it" (John 1:5). We are people of hope and the Bridegroom is preparing a great springtime for his Bride (see Song of Songs 2:11–13). How do we pass over from this winter to the promised springtime? If we can recognize in the above the diagnosis of what ails the modern world, we can also recognize the cure. Here it is: We must recover a sense of *primordial wonder* at the divinely inspired beauty of the human body; we must come to recognize in the human body the revelation of the human *person* whose dignity demands he never be used, exploited, manipulated, or discarded; we must rediscover *the treasure* of human sexuality and gender as a stupendous sign of the divine image in man, and as an invitation to use our freedom to live this divine image through the sincere gift of one's life in marriage or in celibacy for the kingdom. And we do all of the above precisely by pondering the profound understanding of masculinity and femininity found in divine revelation, found in God's Word . . . *made flesh* in Christ.

This is what St. John Paul II's Theology of the Body *is*. And you are now part of a microscopic percentage of people on this planet who have been exposed to it. What will you do with that responsibility? What will you do with the seeds that have fallen to you? I appeal to you, do not let the birds of the air eat them. Do not let the seeds die for lack of moisture. Do not let the cares of this world choke them off (see Luke 8:4–15). Tend to the soil and water the seeds by taking up a further, more in-depth study of the Theology of the Body. Make it your mission in life to learn, live, and share the "Gospel of the body" with everyone you know. Here are a few suggestions for next steps:

- If you have the aptitude, read John Paul II's actual text: *Man and Woman He Created Them: A Theology of the Body* (Pauline, 2006). If you need help with that, read it in conjunction with my extended commentary *Theology of the Body Explained* (Pauline, 2007).

- Explore what other authors and teachers have written about the TOB. Search "theology of the body resources" to find them.

- If you like my approach, visit my ministry's website, corproject.com, and click on "shop" for a full listing of additional resources.

- If you would like ongoing formation in the TOB, consider joining a worldwide community of men and women who are learning, living, and sharing the TOB as members of the Cor Project. Visit cormembership.com to learn more.

- Consider taking a five-day "Immersion Course" through the Theology of the Body Institute. I teach these courses about four times a year. Learn more at tobinstitute.org.

If this Theology of the Body provides the answer to the crisis of our times, it's not because it offers the world some "great teaching." Rather, it's because it reconnects the modern world with the "great mystery" that is Christ and his love for his

Bride, the Church. "We are certainly not seduced by the naive expectation that, faced with the great challenges of our time, we shall find some magic formula. No, we shall not be saved by a formula, but by a Person, and the assurance which he gives us: *I am with you!*"[115]

Christ the Bridegroom is with us, and he is "coming soon" in all his glory (see Revelation 22:7). *This* is what enables us to endure all that is happening in our world right now. The meaning of the body, of sexuality, gender, marriage, and the family is being put on trial, condemned, mocked, rejected, spat upon, scourged, and crucified. But give it "three days" and watch what happens: "On the third day there was a marriage at Cana" (John 2:1). Jesus and Mary are always about the business of restoring God's wine to man and woman's relationship! This is our living hope. This is the hope offered in St. John Paul II's Theology of the Body. If we share this hope with the world, we shall not fall short of renewing the face of the earth.

The Spirit and the Bride say, "Come!" And let him who hears say, "Come!" And let him who is thirsty come, let him who desires take the water of life without price. (Revelation 22:17)

ABOUT THE AUTHOR

Christopher West is a proud husband and father of five. He is also the world's most recognized teacher and promoter of St. John Paul II's Theology of the Body. As founder and president of the Cor Project, he leads a global outreach and membership organization devoted to helping others learn, live, and share this liberating teaching. He is also a cofounder of the Theology of the Body Institute; the intensive courses he teaches there attract students from around the world. His extensive lecturing and numerous best-selling books, articles, and video programs have sparked an international groundswell of interest in the Theology of the Body, and his work has been featured in the *New York Times*; on ABC News, Fox News, and MSNBC; and in countless Catholic and Protestant media outlets.

ENDORSEMENTS

"In a culture still haunted by Gnosticism, where a wedge is so often placed between matter and spirit, soul and body, leading to distortions in our understanding of the human person, Saint John Paul II's Theology of the Body is both much needed and prophetic. I'm grateful to Christopher West for making these teachings accessible to a general audience. This book offers a clear, succinct presentation of Saint John Paul II's important ideas and is a helpful and necessary resource for catechists, evangelists, indeed all people."

—Bishop Robert Barron, Auxiliary Bishop of Los Angeles and founder of Word on Fire

"Theology of the Body for Beginners offers a fresh perspective on this rich seam of human and divine wisdom which Saint John Paul II has left us as his gift. Cynical and utilitarian views of sexuality can easily fall prey to the temptation of misrepresenting its sacredness. They can blind us to God's creative plan for human beings as male and female, to the inherent sacramental logic of our existence and to the ultimate fulfillment which all sexual longing seeks. This book delves beneath the superficial to discover the deepest meaning of human sexuality. But beware: You will find Christopher West's presentation both enlightening and challenging!"

—Archbishop Eamon Martin, Archbishop of Armagh Ireland

NOTES

1. Christopher West, *Fill These Hearts: God, Sex, and the Universal Longing* (New York: Image, 2013), p. 23.

2. My thanks to the late Monsignor Lorenzo Albacete for sharing a version of this story with me when I was in graduate school. It's loosely based on an actual encounter that took place between an Italian priest (Monsignor Giussani) and some starstruck lovers.

3. John Paul II actually divided his manuscript into 135 talks. However, some of the content of his reflections on the Song of Songs was considered too "delicate" for the Wednesday audience format, so he condensed 10 talks in that section to four, thus delivering only 129. For an extended treatment of the undelivered talks, see my book *Heaven's Song* (Ascension Press, 2008).

4. George Weigel, *Witness to Hope* (New York: HarperCollins, 1999), pp. 336, 343, 853.

5. Pope Francis, *Praise Be to You* (North Palm Beach, Fla.: Beacon Publishing), p. 81.

6. Pope Francis, *The Joy of Love* (North Palm Beach, Fla.: Beacon Publishing), p. 117.

7. John Paul II, *Crossing the Threshold of Hope* (New York: Alfred A. Knopf, 1994), p 66.

8. John Paul II, *Mulieris Dignitatem,* 26 (Boston: Pauline Books and Media, 1988).

9. Pope Francis, *The Joy of Love*, 13.

10. Pope Francis, *The Joy of Love*, 142.

11. Pope Benedict XVI, *Deus Caritas Est*, 9 (Boston: Pauline Books and Media, 2006).

12. Pope Benedict XVI, *Deus Caritas Est*, 10.

13. St. Bonaventure, *Bringing Forth Christ: Five Feasts of the Child Jesus* (Oxford, UK: Fairacres Publication, 1884).

14. St. Augustine, Sermon 291.

15. John Paul II, *Letter to Families*, 19 (Boston: Pauline Books and Media, 1994).

16. See John Paul II, *Novo Millennio Ineunte*, 33 (Boston: Pauline Books and Media, 2001).

17. Henry Dieterich, *Through the Year with Bishop Fulton Sheen* (San Francisco: Ignatius Press, 2003), p. 60.

18. Pope Benedict XVI, Lenten Message 2007.

19. John Paul II, *Mulieris Dignitatem*, 26.

20. "The Church Must Guide the Sexual Revolution," interview with Stanislaw Grygiel, retrieved from www.ewtn.com/library/Theology/ZSEXREV.HTM.

21. John Paul II, *Letter to Families*, 23.

22. Karol Wojtyla, *Love and Responsibility* (San Francisco: Ignatius Press, 1993), p.66.

23. John Paul II, *Evangelium Vitae*, 97 (Boston: Pauline Books and Media, 1995).

24. *Gaudium et Spes*, The Second Vatican Council's Pastoral Constitution on the Church in the Modern World, 22 (Boston: Pauline Books and Media, 1965).

25. John Paul II, *Familiaris Consortio*, 11 (Boston: Pauline Books and Media, 1981).

26. Pope Francis, Homily, February 22, 2014.

27. Benedict XVI, Homily, Vatican Basilica, January 6, 2013.

28. Pope Francis, *The Joy of Love*, 56.

29. Karol Wojtyla, *Love and Responsibility*, p.47.

30. Pope Benedict XVI, *Deus Caritas Est*, 9.

31. Pope Francis, *The Joy of Love*, 11.

32. Pope Francis, *The Joy of Love*, 314.

33. Homily, April 15, 2015.

34. Papal audience, December 30, 1981.

35. *Gaudium et Spes*, 24.

36. Benedict XVI, General Audience, November 7, 2012.

37. Raniero Cantalamessa, "The Two Faces of Love," First Lenten Sermon to the Roman Curia, 2011.

38. Benedict XVI, *Deus Caritas Est*, 4.

39. Benedict XVI, *Light of the World* (Ignatius Press, 2010), p. 61.

40. Pope Francis, *The Joy of Love*, 148.

41. Pope Francis, *Evangelii Gaudium*, 39 (Boston: Pauline Books and Media, 2013).

42. John Paul II, *Veritatis Splendor*, 18 (Boston: Pauline Books and Media, 1993).

43. John Paul II, *Dominum et Vivificantem*, 51 (Boston: Pauline Books and Media, 1986).

44. Pope Francis, *The Joy of Love*, 317.

45. Karol Wojtyla, *Love and Responsibility*, pp. 170–171.

46. John Paul II, *Veritatis Splendor*, 15.

47. Alexander Men, *Son of Man* (Torrance, Calif.: Oakwood Publications, 1998), p. 93.

48. John Paul II, April 13, 1994.

49. John Paul II, *Veritatis Splendor*, 103.

50. Karol Wojtyla, *Love and Responsibility*, pp. 190–191.

51. John Paul II, *Orientale Lumen*, 3 (Boston: Pauline Books and Media, 1995).

52. See John Paul II, *Dominum et Vivificantem*, 51.

53. C. S. Lewis, *The Great Divorce* (New York: Macmillan, 1946), p. 104.

54. Benedict XVI, *Spe Salvi*, 1 (Boston: Pauline Books and Media, 2007).

55. St. Bonaventure, *De Assumptione B. Mariae Virginis*, Sermo 1

56. Peter Kreeft, *Everything You Ever Wanted to Know about Heaven* (San Francisco: Ignatius Press, 1990), p. 93.

57. Dennis Kinlaw, *Let's Start with Jesus* (Grand Rapids, Mich.: Zondervan, 2005), p. 62.

58. Pope Francis, October 15, 2014.

59. Benedict XVI, November 7, 2012.

60. *Gaudium et Spes*, 24.

61. Benedict XVI, *Deus Caritas Est*, 9, 10.

62. Benedict XVI, *Deus Caritas Est*, 4.

63. Pope Francis, *Evangelii Gaudium*, 3.

64. Benedict XVI, *Deus Caritas Est*, 1.

65. John Paul II, *Novo Millennio Ineunte*, 33 (Boston: Pauline Books and Media, 2001).

66. Benedict XVI, *Spe Salvi*, 1 (Boston: Pauline Books and Media, 2007).

67. John Paul II, *Novo Millennio Ineunte*, 33.

68. Pope Francis, April 22, 2013.

69. John Paul II, *Familiaris Consortio*, 11.

70. John Paul II included his reflections on "celibacy for the kingdom" in the context of his reflection on the resurrection

of the body. Here, I have given his treatment of the subject its own chapter.

71. John Paul II, *Familiaris Consortio*, 16.

72. Karol Wojtyla, *Love and Responsibility*, p. 254.

73. Karol Wojtyla, *Love and Responsibility*, p. 255.

74. Christopher West, *Good News about Sex & Marriage* (Cincinnati: Servant, 2004), p. 167.

75. Raniero Cantalamessa, "The Two Faces of Love."

76. Benedict XVI, *Deus Caritas Est*, 9, 10.

77. Pope Francis, *The Joy of Love*, 161.

78. Karol Wojtyla, *Love and Responsibility*, p. 140.

79. John Paul II, *Letter to Families*, 19 (Boston: Pauline Books and Media, 1994).

80. Karol Wojtyla, *Love and Responsibility*, pp. 272, 275.

81. John Paul II, *Mulieris Dignitatem*, 27.

82. John Paul II, *Redemptor Hominis*, 1 (Boston: Pauline and Media, 1979)

83. Pope Francis, *The Joy of Love*, 73.

84. Benedict XVI, January 31, 2007.

85. Karol Wojtyla, *Love and Responsibility*, p. 135.

86. Pope Francis, *The Joy of Love*, 74.

87. Richard A. Norris, trans. and ed., *The Song of Songs as Interpreted by Early Christian and Medieval Commentators* (Grand Rapids, Mich.: Eerdmans, 2003), p. 18.

88. Richard A. Norris, *The Song of Songs as Interpreted by Early Christian and Medieval Commentators*, p. 18.

89. Benedict XVI, *Deus Caritas Est*, 10.

90. Pope Francis, *The Joy of Love*, 316.

91. John Paul II, *Familiaris Consortio*, 13.

92. Christopher West, *Heaven's Song: Sexual Love as It Was Meant

to Be (West Chester, Penn.: Ascension Press, 2008), p. 130.

93. Joseph Ratzinger, *The Spirit of the Liturgy* (San Francisco: Ignatius Press, 2000), p. 197.

94. Pope Francis, *The Joy of Love*, 122.

95. Pope Francis, *The Joy of Love*, 284.

96. Pope Francis, *Praise Be to You*, 112.

97. Pope Francis, *The Joy of the Gospel*, 34 (North Palm Beach, Fla.: Beacon Publishing, 2014).

98. Pope Francis, *The Joy of the Gospel*, 39.

99. Raniero Cantalamessa, "The Two Faces of Love."

100. Pope Francis, cited in *Magnificat*, Oct. 13, 2013.

101. John Paul II, *Veritatis Splendor*, 23.

102. Pope Francis, *The Joy of the Gospel*, 153.

103. Sigmund Freud, *Introductory Lectures in Psycho-Analysis* (New York: W. W. Norton, 1990).

104. Paul VI, *Humanae Vitae*, 7; http://w2.vatican.va/content/paul-vi/en/encyclicals/documents/hf_p-vi_enc_25071968_humanae-vitae.html.

105. Pope Francis, *The Joy of the Gospel*, 172.

106. Pope Francis, *The Joy of Love*, 80.

107. Paul VI, *Humanae Vitae*, 10.

108. John Paul II, *Familiaris Consortio*, 32.

109. John Paul II, October 10, 1983.

110. John Paul II, *Gaudium et Spes*, 51.

111. Karl Wojtyla, *Love and Responsibility*, p. 167.

112. Pope Francis, *The Joy of the Gospel*, 171.

113. "Theology of the Body," lecture by Monsignor Lorenzo Albacete at the University of San Francisco (Flocchini Forum, 1995).

John Paul II, *Letter to Families*, 19.

100. John Paul II, *Novo Millennio Ineunte*, 29.

JOIN OUR COMMUNITY

BECOME A PATRON OF THE
THEOLOGY OF THE BODY INSTITUTE COMMUNITY
AND HELP US SPREAD JOHN PAUL II'S
LIBERATING MESSAGE AROUND THE WORLD.

AS A PATRON...

- *YOU MAKE OUR WORK POSSIBLE.*
- *YOU ARE PART OF A COMMUNITY.*
- *YOU ARE A DEFENDER OF TRUTH.*
- *YOU ARE A GIFT TO US.*

OUR GIFT TO YOU

- *ACCESS TO ONLINE COMMUNITY.*
- *VIDEO FORMATION.*
- *DEDICATED SUPPORT.*
- *PRINTABLE STUDY GUIDES.*
- *OTHER GREAT PERKS AS A PATRON!*

DR. CHRISTOPHER WEST, *TOBI PRESIDENT*

BECOME A PATRON AT
WWW.TOBPATRON.COM

@CWESTOFFICIAL
@TOBINSTITUTE

CHRISTOPHER WEST
ASKCHRISTOPHERWEST.COM
TOBINSTITUTE.ORG

HAVE YOU EVER WONDERED HOW THE CATHOLIC FAITH COULD HELP YOU LIVE BETTER?

How it could help you find more *joy* at work, *manage* your personal finances, *improve* your marriage, or make you a *better* parent?

THERE IS GENIUS IN CATHOLICISM.

When *Catholicism* is lived as it is intended to be, it elevates every part of our lives. It may sound simple, but they say *genius is taking something complex and making it simple.*

Dynamic Catholic started with a dream: to help ordinary people discover the *genius of Catholicism.*

Wherever you are in your journey, we want to meet you there and walk with you, *step by step,* helping you to discover God and become *the-best-version-of-yourself.*

To find more helpful resources, visit us online at DynamicCatholic.com.

Dynamic Catholic

FEED YOUR SOUL